55 Southern States
Recipes for Home

By: Kelly Johnson

Table of Contents

Appetizers:

- Pimento Cheese Ball
- Fried Pickles with Buttermilk Ranch
- Southern Caviar (Black-yed Pea Dip)
- Cornbread Muffins with Honey Butter
- Bacon-wrapped **Jalapeño Poppers**

Soups and Stews:

- Kentucky Bourbon Chili
- Grits and Greens Soup
- Louisiana Seafood Gumbo
- Tomato and Okra Stew
- White Bean and Ham Soup

Main Dishes:

- Shrimp and Grits
- Chicken and Waffles
- Mississippi Roast
- Texas BBQ Brisket
- Carolina Pulled Pork
- Alabama Fried Catfish
- Kentucky Hot Brown
- Tennessee Hot Chicken

Side Dishes:

- Collard Greens with Ham Hocks
- Southern Corn Pudding
- Baked Macaroni and Cheese
- Fried Okra
- Candied Sweet Potatoes
- Creamed Corn
- Red Beans and Rice

Breads:
- Buttermilk Biscuits
- Southern Cornbread
- Hoppin' John Cornbread
- Sweet Potato Biscuits
- Parker House Rolls

Salads:
- Southern Cobb Salad
- Classic Potato Salad
- Fried Green Tomato Salad
- Watermelon and Feta Salad
- Shrimp Remoulade Salad

Casseroles:
- Chicken and Rice Casserole
- Grits Casserole
- Squash Casserole
- Baked Chicken and Cornbread Dressing
- Crawfish Étouffée Casserole

Desserts:
- Pecan Pie
- Peach Cobbler
- Banana Pudding
- Red Velvet Cake
- Bourbon Bread Pudding

Drinks:
- Sweet Tea
- Mint Julep
- Southern Comfort Punch
- Arnold Palmer (Half-and-Half)
- Mississippi Mudslide (Chocolate Milkshake with Bourbon)

Breakfast/Brunch:

- Biscuits and Gravy
- Shrimp and Grits Breakfast Casserole
- Southern-style Breakfast Burrito
- Grits and Grillades
- Louisiana Beignets

Appetizers:

Pimento Cheese Ball

Ingredients:

- 8 oz cream cheese, softened
- 2 cups sharp cheddar cheese, shredded
- 1/2 cup mayonnaise
- 1/4 cup diced pimentos, drained
- 1/4 cup green onions, finely chopped
- 1/4 teaspoon garlic powder
- 1/4 teaspoon onion powder
- 1/4 teaspoon cayenne pepper (optional, for a bit of heat)
- Salt and black pepper to taste
- 1 cup chopped pecans or walnuts, for coating

Instructions:

In a large mixing bowl, combine the softened cream cheese, shredded cheddar cheese, mayonnaise, diced pimentos, green onions, garlic powder, onion powder, and cayenne pepper.

Mix the ingredients together until well combined. You can use a hand mixer or mix by hand.

Season the mixture with salt and black pepper to taste. Keep in mind that the cheese can be salty, so adjust accordingly.

Once the mixture is well combined and seasoned, shape it into a ball. You can use plastic wrap to help form a smooth ball shape.

In a separate plate, spread out the chopped nuts. Roll the cheese ball in the nuts until it is fully coated.

Wrap the cheese ball in plastic wrap and refrigerate for at least 1-2 hours, or overnight if possible. This allows the flavors to meld and the cheese ball to firm up.

Before serving, let the cheese ball sit at room temperature for about 15-20 minutes to soften slightly. Serve with crackers, pretzels, or sliced vegetables.

Enjoy your delicious Pimento Cheese Ball as a flavorful and crowd-pleasing appetizer!

Fried Pickles with Buttermilk Ranch

Ingredients:

For the Fried Pickles:

- 1 cup dill pickle chips, drained
- 1 cup buttermilk
- 1 cup all-purpose flour
- 1 teaspoon garlic powder
- 1 teaspoon paprika
- 1/2 teaspoon cayenne pepper (adjust to taste)
- Salt and black pepper to taste
- Vegetable oil for frying

For the Buttermilk Ranch Dip:

- 1 cup mayonnaise
- 1/2 cup buttermilk
- 1 tablespoon fresh chives, finely chopped
- 1 tablespoon fresh parsley, finely chopped
- 1 teaspoon dried dill
- 1 teaspoon garlic powder
- Salt and black pepper to taste

Instructions:

For the Fried Pickles:

In a bowl, soak the pickle chips in buttermilk for at least 30 minutes.
In a separate bowl, combine flour, garlic powder, paprika, cayenne pepper, salt, and black pepper.
Heat vegetable oil in a deep fryer or large, deep skillet to 375°F (190°C).
Dredge each pickle chip in the flour mixture, ensuring they are well coated.
Fry the coated pickles in batches until golden brown, usually 2-3 minutes per batch. Use a slotted spoon to remove them from the oil and place them on paper towels to drain excess oil.
Repeat until all pickle chips are fried.

For the Buttermilk Ranch Dip:

In a bowl, whisk together mayonnaise, buttermilk, chives, parsley, dried dill, and garlic powder.

Season with salt and black pepper to taste. Adjust the herbs and seasoning according to your preferences.

Refrigerate the ranch dip for at least 30 minutes before serving to allow the flavors to meld.

Serve the crispy Fried Pickles with the Buttermilk Ranch Dip on the side. Enjoy the delightful combination of crunchy pickles and tangy ranch!

Southern Caviar (Black-yed Pea Dip)

Ingredients:

- 2 cans (15 oz each) black-eyed peas, drained and rinsed
- 1 cup corn kernels (fresh, frozen, or canned)
- 1 red bell pepper, finely diced
- 1/2 red onion, finely diced
- 2 cloves garlic, minced
- 1/4 cup fresh cilantro, chopped
- 1 jalapeño pepper, seeds removed and finely diced (adjust to taste)
- Juice of 2 limes
- 1/4 cup extra-virgin olive oil
- 1 teaspoon ground cumin
- Salt and black pepper to taste
- Tortilla chips or crackers for serving

Instructions:

In a large bowl, combine the black-eyed peas, corn, diced red bell pepper, diced red onion, minced garlic, chopped cilantro, and finely diced jalapeño.
In a small bowl, whisk together the lime juice, extra-virgin olive oil, ground cumin, salt, and black pepper.
Pour the dressing over the black-eyed pea mixture and gently toss everything together until well combined.
Cover the bowl and refrigerate the Southern Caviar for at least 2 hours to allow the flavors to meld.
Before serving, give the dip a gentle stir and taste for seasoning, adjusting salt and pepper if necessary.
Serve the Southern Caviar with tortilla chips or crackers.

This refreshing and flavorful Black-eyed Pea Dip is a perfect addition to any

Southern-inspired gathering or as a tasty snack for any occasion!

Cornbread Muffins with Honey Butter

Ingredients:

For Cornbread Muffins:

- 1 cup cornmeal
- 1 cup all-purpose flour
- 1 tablespoon baking powder
- 1/2 teaspoon baking soda
- 1/2 teaspoon salt
- 1 cup buttermilk
- 1/2 cup unsalted butter, melted and cooled
- 1/4 cup honey
- 2 large eggs

For Honey Butter:

- 1/2 cup unsalted butter, softened
- 2 tablespoons honey
- Pinch of salt (optional)

Instructions:

For Cornbread Muffins:

Preheat your oven to 375°F (190°C). Grease a muffin tin or line it with paper liners.
In a large bowl, whisk together the cornmeal, all-purpose flour, baking powder, baking soda, and salt.
In another bowl, whisk together the buttermilk, melted butter, honey, and eggs.
Pour the wet ingredients into the dry ingredients and stir until just combined. Do not overmix; a few lumps are okay.
Divide the batter evenly among the muffin cups, filling each about 2/3 full.
Bake for 15-18 minutes or until a toothpick inserted into the center of a muffin comes out clean.
Allow the muffins to cool in the tin for a few minutes before transferring them to a wire rack to cool completely.

For Honey Butter:

In a small bowl, whip together softened butter, honey, and a pinch of salt (if desired) until well combined.
Taste and adjust the sweetness or saltiness according to your preference.
Serve the Cornbread Muffins warm with a dollop of Honey Butter on top.

These Cornbread Muffins with Honey Butter are a delightful combination of sweet and savory, making them a perfect side for soups, stews, or as a tasty snack on their own!

Bacon-wrapped Jalapeño Poppers

Ingredients:

- 12 large jalapeño peppers, halved lengthwise and seeds removed
- 8 oz cream cheese, softened
- 1 cup shredded cheddar cheese
- 1 teaspoon garlic powder
- 1/2 teaspoon onion powder
- 12 slices of bacon, cut in half
- Toothpicks

Instructions:

Preheat your oven to 375°F (190°C). Line a baking sheet with parchment paper.
In a bowl, combine the softened cream cheese, shredded cheddar cheese, garlic powder, and onion powder. Mix until well combined.
Fill each jalapeño half with the cream cheese mixture, smoothing the top with a spoon.
Wrap each stuffed jalapeño with a half-slice of bacon, securing it with a toothpick. Ensure the toothpick goes through the bacon and into the pepper to hold everything in place.
Place the bacon-wrapped jalapeño poppers on the prepared baking sheet.
Bake in the preheated oven for about 20-25 minutes or until the bacon is crispy and the peppers are tender.
If you prefer a crispier bacon, you can broil the poppers for an additional 2-3 minutes, but keep a close eye on them to prevent burning.
Remove from the oven and let them cool for a few minutes before serving.

These Bacon-wrapped Jalapeño Poppers are a crowd-pleasing appetizer, combining the heat of jalapeños with the creamy richness of cream cheese and the savory goodness of bacon. Enjoy them at your next gathering!

Soups and Stews:

Kentucky Bourbon Chili

Ingredients:

- 2 pounds ground beef
- 1 large onion, diced
- 3 cloves garlic, minced
- 2 cans (14 oz each) diced tomatoes, undrained
- 1 can (6 oz) tomato paste
- 1 can (15 oz) kidney beans, drained and rinsed
- 1 can (15 oz) black beans, drained and rinsed
- 1/4 cup bourbon
- 2 tablespoons chili powder
- 1 tablespoon cumin
- 1 teaspoon smoked paprika
- 1/2 teaspoon cayenne pepper (adjust to taste)
- Salt and black pepper to taste
- 1 cup beef broth
- 2 tablespoons Worcestershire sauce
- 1 tablespoon brown sugar
- Chopped green onions, shredded cheese, and sour cream for garnish

Instructions:

In a large pot or Dutch oven, brown the ground beef over medium heat. Drain any excess fat.
Add the diced onion and minced garlic to the pot. Cook for about 5 minutes until the onion is softened.
Stir in the bourbon, scraping the bottom of the pot to release any browned bits.
Add diced tomatoes, tomato paste, kidney beans, black beans, chili powder, cumin, smoked paprika, cayenne pepper, salt, and black pepper. Mix well.
Pour in the beef broth and Worcestershire sauce. Stir in the brown sugar.
Bring the chili to a simmer, then reduce the heat to low. Cover and let it simmer for at least 1 hour, stirring occasionally.
Taste and adjust the seasoning as needed. If you prefer a thicker chili, let it simmer uncovered for an additional 15-20 minutes.

Serve the Kentucky Bourbon Chili hot, garnished with chopped green onions, shredded cheese, and a dollop of sour cream.

This Kentucky Bourbon Chili is rich and flavorful, with a touch of bourbon adding a unique twist to the classic comfort food. Enjoy it with your favorite cornbread or crackers!

Grits and Greens Soup

Ingredients:

- 1 cup stone-ground grits
- 4 cups chicken or vegetable broth
- 1 bunch collard greens, stems removed and leaves chopped
- 1 large onion, finely chopped
- 3 cloves garlic, minced
- 1 cup diced smoked ham or bacon (optional)
- 2 tablespoons olive oil
- 1 teaspoon smoked paprika
- Salt and black pepper to taste
- Hot sauce (optional, for serving)
- Chopped green onions for garnish

Instructions:

In a medium saucepan, bring the broth to a boil. Gradually whisk in the grits, reduce the heat to low, cover, and simmer for about 20-25 minutes or until the grits are tender, stirring occasionally.
While the grits are cooking, heat olive oil in a large pot over medium heat. Add the chopped onion and cook until softened, about 5 minutes.
Add minced garlic to the pot and cook for an additional 1-2 minutes until fragrant.
If using, add diced smoked ham or bacon to the pot and cook until browned.
Stir in the chopped collard greens and cook until wilted, about 3-5 minutes.
Sprinkle smoked paprika over the greens, season with salt and black pepper to taste, and stir to combine.
Pour the cooked grits into the pot with the greens and stir until well combined. Taste and adjust the seasoning as needed. If the soup is too thick, you can add more broth to achieve your desired consistency.
Serve the Grits and Greens Soup hot, with a dash of hot sauce if you like, and garnish with chopped green onions.

This hearty and flavorful Grits and Greens Soup combines the creaminess of grits with the earthy taste of collard greens for a comforting Southern experience. Enjoy it as a satisfying meal on its own or as a side dish!

Louisiana Seafood Gumbo

Ingredients:

For the Roux:

- 1 cup all-purpose flour
- 1 cup vegetable oil

For the Gumbo:

- 1 cup onion, finely chopped
- 1 cup bell pepper, finely chopped
- 1 cup celery, finely chopped
- 3 cloves garlic, minced
- 1 pound andouille sausage, sliced
- 1/2 cup vegetable oil
- 8 cups seafood or chicken broth
- 1 pound shrimp, peeled and deveined
- 1 pound crab meat
- 1 pound okra, sliced (fresh or frozen)
- 1 can (14 oz) diced tomatoes, undrained
- 1 tablespoon Worcestershire sauce
- 1 teaspoon hot sauce (adjust to taste)
- 2 bay leaves
- 1 teaspoon dried thyme
- Salt and black pepper to taste
- 1/4 cup fresh parsley, chopped
- 1/4 cup green onions, chopped
- Cooked white rice for serving

Instructions:

For the Roux:

In a heavy-bottomed pot, combine the flour and oil over medium heat to make the roux. Stir continuously to avoid burning.
Continue to cook the roux, stirring constantly, until it reaches a dark brown color, resembling the color of chocolate. Be patient; this may take 20-30 minutes.

For the Gumbo:

Once the roux is dark brown, add chopped onions, bell peppers, celery, and minced garlic. Stir well and cook for about 5-7 minutes until the vegetables are softened.
In a separate skillet, sauté the andouille sausage slices until browned. Drain any excess fat.
Add the sausage to the pot with the roux and vegetables.
Gradually pour in the seafood or chicken broth while stirring to avoid lumps. Bring the mixture to a simmer.
Add the sliced okra, diced tomatoes, Worcestershire sauce, hot sauce, bay leaves, dried thyme, salt, and black pepper. Simmer for about 30 minutes, stirring occasionally.
Add the shrimp and crab meat to the pot. Cook for an additional 10-15 minutes until the seafood is cooked through.
Taste and adjust the seasoning. Remove the bay leaves.
Just before serving, stir in chopped parsley and green onions.
Serve the Louisiana Seafood Gumbo over cooked white rice.

Enjoy this rich and authentic Louisiana Seafood Gumbo, a true Southern classic with a delightful mix of flavors!

Tomato and Okra Stew

Ingredients:

- 2 tablespoons vegetable oil
- 1 onion, finely chopped
- 2 cloves garlic, minced
- 1 pound okra, sliced
- 4 cups fresh or canned diced tomatoes
- 1 bell pepper, diced
- 1 celery stalk, diced
- 1 teaspoon dried thyme
- 1 teaspoon dried oregano
- 1 teaspoon smoked paprika
- 1 bay leaf
- Salt and black pepper to taste
- Dash of hot sauce (optional)
- Chopped fresh parsley for garnish

Instructions:

In a large pot, heat vegetable oil over medium heat. Add chopped onions and garlic, sautéing until onions are translucent.
Add sliced okra to the pot and cook for about 5-7 minutes until it starts to soften.
Stir in diced tomatoes, bell pepper, and celery. Allow the mixture to come to a simmer.
Add dried thyme, dried oregano, smoked paprika, bay leaf, salt, and black pepper to the pot. Stir well to combine.
If using, add a dash of hot sauce for some heat. Adjust according to your spice preference.
Cover the pot and let the stew simmer on low heat for about 20-25 minutes, stirring occasionally.
Taste and adjust the seasoning as needed. Remove the bay leaf.
Serve the Tomato and Okra Stew hot, garnished with chopped fresh parsley.

This Tomato and Okra Stew is a wonderful combination of flavors and textures. Enjoy it as a side dish or a light vegetarian main course. It pairs well with rice, quinoa, or crusty bread.

White Bean and Ham Soup

Ingredients:

- 1 pound dried white beans (Great Northern or Navy), soaked overnight and drained
- 2 tablespoons olive oil
- 1 onion, diced
- 2 carrots, diced
- 2 celery stalks, diced
- 3 cloves garlic, minced
- 1 pound ham hocks or ham bone
- 8 cups chicken or vegetable broth
- 2 bay leaves
- 1 teaspoon dried thyme
- Salt and black pepper to taste
- 2 cups cooked ham, diced
- 1 cup frozen or fresh spinach (optional)
- Fresh parsley for garnish

Instructions:

In a large pot, heat olive oil over medium heat. Add diced onions, carrots, and celery. Sauté until the vegetables are softened, about 5-7 minutes.
Add minced garlic and cook for an additional 1-2 minutes until fragrant.
Add soaked and drained white beans to the pot, along with ham hocks or ham bone.
Pour in the chicken or vegetable broth, and add bay leaves and dried thyme.
Season with salt and black pepper to taste.
Bring the soup to a boil, then reduce the heat to low. Cover and simmer for about 1 to 1.5 hours, or until the beans are tender.
Remove the ham hocks or bone from the pot. If using ham hocks, shred the meat and return it to the pot. Discard the bone.
Add diced cooked ham to the soup and stir to combine. If using spinach, add it to the soup and cook until wilted.
Taste and adjust the seasoning as needed. Remove the bay leaves.
Serve the White Bean and Ham Soup hot, garnished with fresh parsley.

This hearty and comforting White Bean and Ham Soup is perfect for a cozy meal, especially during colder weather. Enjoy it with crusty bread or a side salad!

Main Dishes:

Shrimp and Grits

Ingredients:

For the Grits:

- 1 cup stone-ground grits
- 4 cups water or chicken broth
- Salt and black pepper to taste
- 1 cup shredded cheddar cheese (optional)
- 2 tablespoons unsalted butter

For the Shrimp:

- 1 pound large shrimp, peeled and deveined
- 1 tablespoon Cajun seasoning
- Salt and black pepper to taste
- 2 tablespoons olive oil
- 4 cloves garlic, minced
- 1 cup cherry tomatoes, halved
- 1/2 cup chicken broth
- 1/4 cup fresh parsley, chopped
- Juice of 1 lemon

Instructions:

For the Grits:

In a medium saucepan, bring water or chicken broth to a boil. Gradually whisk in the grits, reduce the heat to low, cover, and simmer for about 20-25 minutes or until the grits are tender, stirring occasionally.
Season the cooked grits with salt and black pepper. If desired, stir in shredded cheddar cheese and butter until melted and smooth.

For the Shrimp:

In a bowl, toss the peeled and deveined shrimp with Cajun seasoning, salt, and black pepper, ensuring they are well coated.

Heat olive oil in a large skillet over medium-high heat. Add the seasoned shrimp and cook for 2-3 minutes per side or until they turn pink and opaque. Remove the shrimp from the skillet and set aside.

In the same skillet, add minced garlic and cook for about 1 minute until fragrant. Add cherry tomatoes to the skillet and cook for 2-3 minutes until they start to soften.

Pour in chicken broth and bring to a simmer. Cook for an additional 2-3 minutes to allow the flavors to meld.

Return the cooked shrimp to the skillet. Add chopped parsley and lemon juice. Toss everything together until well combined and heated through.

Serve the shrimp over a bed of creamy grits.

Enjoy your Shrimp and Grits, a Southern classic known for its delightful combination of savory shrimp and creamy, cheesy grits!

Chicken and Waffles

Ingredients:

For the Fried Chicken:

- 4 boneless, skinless chicken breasts
- 2 cups buttermilk
- 2 cups all-purpose flour
- 1 teaspoon salt
- 1 teaspoon black pepper
- 1 teaspoon paprika
- 1 teaspoon garlic powder
- 1 teaspoon onion powder
- Vegetable oil for frying

For the Waffles:

- 2 cups all-purpose flour
- 2 tablespoons sugar
- 1 tablespoon baking powder
- 1/2 teaspoon salt
- 2 large eggs
- 1 3/4 cups milk
- 1/2 cup unsalted butter, melted
- 1 teaspoon vanilla extract

For Serving:

- Maple syrup
- Hot sauce (optional)

Instructions:

For the Fried Chicken:

Marinate the chicken breasts in buttermilk for at least 2 hours or overnight in the refrigerator.
In a shallow dish, combine flour, salt, black pepper, paprika, garlic powder, and onion powder.

Heat vegetable oil in a deep fryer or a large, deep skillet to 350°F (180°C).
Dredge each chicken breast in the seasoned flour mixture, ensuring they are well coated.
Fry the coated chicken breasts for 12-15 minutes or until golden brown and cooked through. Ensure the internal temperature reaches 165°F (74°C).
Place the fried chicken on a paper towel-lined plate to drain excess oil.

For the Waffles:

Preheat your waffle iron according to the manufacturer's instructions.
In a large bowl, whisk together flour, sugar, baking powder, and salt.
In another bowl, whisk together eggs, milk, melted butter, and vanilla extract.
Pour the wet ingredients into the dry ingredients and stir until just combined. Do not overmix; a few lumps are okay.
Cook the waffle batter according to your waffle iron instructions until golden brown and crisp.

For Serving:

Serve each fried chicken breast on top of a waffle.
Drizzle with maple syrup and, if desired, add a touch of hot sauce for a spicy kick.

Enjoy your delicious Chicken and Waffles, a perfect blend of savory and sweet that's popular in Southern cuisine!

Mississippi Roast

Ingredients:

- 1 (3-4 pounds) chuck roast
- 1 packet (1 ounce) ranch seasoning mix
- 1 packet (1 ounce) au jus gravy mix
- 1/2 cup unsalted butter
- 5-6 whole pepperoncini peppers
- 1/4 cup pepperoncini pepper juice

Instructions:

Prep the Chuck Roast:
- Pat the chuck roast dry with paper towels.
- Sprinkle the ranch seasoning mix evenly over the roast.
- Do the same with the au jus gravy mix.

Sear the Roast (Optional):
- While this step is optional, it can enhance the flavor. Heat a large skillet or Dutch oven over medium-high heat.
- Add a bit of oil, and sear the chuck roast on all sides until browned. This should take about 2-3 minutes per side.

Slow Cook the Roast:
- Place the chuck roast in the slow cooker.
- Add the unsalted butter, whole pepperoncini peppers, and pepperoncini juice.

Cooking:
- Cover the slow cooker and cook on low for 8 hours or until the meat is tender and easily falls apart.

Shred the Meat:
- Once cooked, use two forks to shred the meat right in the slow cooker. Discard any excess fat.

Serve:
- Serve the shredded Mississippi Roast over rice, mashed potatoes, or in sandwiches.
- Spoon some of the flavorful juices and pepperoncini peppers over the meat.

Garnish (Optional):
- Garnish with additional fresh chopped parsley or chives if desired.

The Mississippi Roast is known for its tangy and savory flavor profile. The combination of ranch seasoning, au jus mix, and the unique addition of pepperoncini peppers creates a delicious and comforting dish. Enjoy!

Texas BBQ Brisket

Ingredients:

For the Brisket:

- 1 whole beef brisket (10-12 pounds)
- 1/4 cup black pepper, coarsely ground
- 1/4 cup kosher salt
- 1/4 cup paprika
- 2 tablespoons brown sugar
- 1 tablespoon chili powder
- 1 tablespoon garlic powder
- 1 tablespoon onion powder
- 1 teaspoon cayenne pepper (adjust to taste)
- Wood chips for smoking (preferably oak or hickory)

For the Mop Sauce:

- 1 cup apple cider vinegar
- 1 cup water
- 1/2 cup vegetable oil
- 2 tablespoons Worcestershire sauce
- 2 tablespoons black pepper, coarsely ground
- 1 tablespoon kosher salt

Instructions:

Prepare the Brisket:
- Trim excess fat from the brisket, leaving about 1/4 inch of fat on the surface.
- In a bowl, mix together the black pepper, kosher salt, paprika, brown sugar, chili powder, garlic powder, onion powder, and cayenne pepper to create the rub.

Apply the Rub:
- Rub the spice mixture generously over the brisket, ensuring an even coating on all sides. Let it sit at room temperature for about 1 hour.

Preheat the Smoker:
- Preheat your smoker to 225°F (107°C). Add wood chips for smoking to enhance the flavor.

Smoke the Brisket:
- Place the brisket on the smoker with the fat side up.
- Smoke the brisket for about 1.5 to 2 hours per pound or until the internal temperature reaches around 200°F (93°C).

Prepare the Mop Sauce:
- While the brisket is smoking, mix together the apple cider vinegar, water, vegetable oil, Worcestershire sauce, black pepper, and kosher salt to create the mop sauce.

Mop the Brisket:
- Every hour during the smoking process, baste the brisket with the mop sauce using a brush or spray bottle.

Rest and Slice:
- Once the brisket reaches the desired temperature, remove it from the smoker.
- Let it rest for at least 30 minutes before slicing. This allows the juices to redistribute, keeping the meat moist.

Slice and Serve:
- Slice the brisket against the grain into 1/4-inch slices.
- Serve with your favorite BBQ sauce, pickles, and bread.

Enjoy your Texas BBQ Brisket, a true Southern barbecue classic with a smoky and flavorful profile!

Carolina Pulled Pork

Ingredients:

For the Pork:

- 1 pork shoulder or pork butt (5-7 pounds)
- 2 tablespoons brown sugar
- 2 tablespoons paprika
- 1 tablespoon salt
- 1 tablespoon black pepper
- 1 tablespoon garlic powder
- 1 tablespoon onion powder
- 1 teaspoon cayenne pepper (adjust to taste)
- 1 cup apple cider vinegar
- 1 cup apple juice or chicken broth

For the Carolina Vinegar Sauce:

- 1 cup apple cider vinegar
- 1 cup water
- 1 tablespoon brown sugar
- 1 tablespoon hot sauce (adjust to taste)
- 1 teaspoon red pepper flakes
- Salt and black pepper to taste

For Serving:

- Hamburger buns or sandwich rolls
- Coleslaw (optional)

Instructions:

Prepare the Pork:
- In a small bowl, combine brown sugar, paprika, salt, black pepper, garlic powder, onion powder, and cayenne pepper to create the dry rub.
- Rub the mixture all over the pork shoulder, ensuring an even coating. Let it marinate in the refrigerator for at least 4 hours or overnight.

Preheat the Smoker or Oven:
- Preheat your smoker or oven to 225°F (107°C).

Smoke or Roast the Pork:
- Place the pork shoulder in the smoker or oven, fat side up.
- Smoke or roast for about 1.5 to 2 hours per pound or until the internal temperature reaches around 195-205°F (90-96°C).

Wrap the Pork:
- If you're using a smoker, you may wrap the pork in foil once it reaches an internal temperature of around 160°F (71°C). This helps speed up the cooking process and keeps the meat moist.

Rest and Shred:
- Once the pork is cooked and tender, let it rest for about 30 minutes.
- Shred the pork using two forks or your hands, discarding any excess fat.

Prepare the Carolina Vinegar Sauce:
- In a saucepan, combine apple cider vinegar, water, brown sugar, hot sauce, red pepper flakes, salt, and black pepper. Bring to a simmer over medium heat, stirring until the sugar dissolves.

Combine the Sauce with the Pulled Pork:
- Pour half of the vinegar sauce over the shredded pork and mix well. Reserve the remaining sauce for serving.

Serve:
- Serve the Carolina Pulled Pork on hamburger buns or sandwich rolls.
- Optionally, top with coleslaw for added freshness and crunch.

Enjoy your Carolina Pulled Pork with its distinctive tangy and vinegar-based flavor!

Alabama Fried Catfish

Ingredients:

For the Catfish:

- 4 catfish fillets
- 1 cup buttermilk
- 1 cup cornmeal
- 1 cup all-purpose flour
- 1 teaspoon salt
- 1 teaspoon black pepper
- 1/2 teaspoon cayenne pepper (adjust to taste)
- Vegetable oil for frying

For the Remoulade Sauce:

- 1 cup mayonnaise
- 2 tablespoons Dijon mustard
- 1 tablespoon sweet pickle relish
- 1 tablespoon chopped fresh parsley
- 1 teaspoon hot sauce (adjust to taste)
- 1 teaspoon lemon juice
- 1 teaspoon Worcestershire sauce
- Salt and black pepper to taste

Instructions:

For the Catfish:

In a shallow dish, soak the catfish fillets in buttermilk for at least 30 minutes. This helps tenderize the fish and adds flavor.

In another shallow dish, mix together cornmeal, all-purpose flour, salt, black pepper, and cayenne pepper to create the coating mixture.

Heat vegetable oil in a large skillet or deep fryer to 350°F (175°C).

Remove the catfish fillets from the buttermilk and dredge them in the cornmeal mixture, ensuring they are well coated.

Fry the catfish fillets in the hot oil for about 4-6 minutes per side, or until they are golden brown and cooked through. The internal temperature should reach 145°F (63°C).

Place the fried catfish on a paper towel-lined plate to absorb any excess oil.

For the Remoulade Sauce:

In a bowl, whisk together mayonnaise, Dijon mustard, sweet pickle relish, chopped fresh parsley, hot sauce, lemon juice, Worcestershire sauce, salt, and black pepper.
Taste the remoulade sauce and adjust the seasoning according to your preference.

Serve:

Serve the Alabama Fried Catfish hot with a side of remoulade sauce for dipping.

Enjoy your crispy and flavorful Alabama Fried Catfish with the zesty kick of remoulade sauce! It's a delightful Southern dish that's perfect for a comforting meal.

Kentucky Hot Brown

Ingredients:

For the Mornay Sauce:

- 2 tablespoons unsalted butter
- 2 tablespoons all-purpose flour
- 2 cups whole milk
- 1 cup shredded sharp cheddar cheese
- 1/2 cup grated Parmesan cheese
- Salt and white pepper to taste
- A pinch of nutmeg

For the Hot Brown:

- 4 slices thick-cut white bread
- 1 pound roasted turkey breast, sliced
- 8 slices cooked bacon
- 2 medium-sized tomatoes, sliced
- Mornay sauce (from the recipe above)
- Paprika for garnish
- Chopped fresh parsley for garnish

Instructions:

For the Mornay Sauce:

In a saucepan, melt the butter over medium heat. Add the flour and whisk constantly to create a roux. Cook for 1-2 minutes.
Gradually whisk in the milk, ensuring there are no lumps. Continue to whisk until the mixture thickens.
Reduce the heat to low, and add the shredded cheddar cheese and grated Parmesan cheese. Stir until the cheese is melted and the sauce is smooth.
Season the Mornay sauce with salt, white pepper, and a pinch of nutmeg. Keep warm over low heat while preparing the rest of the dish.

For the Hot Brown:

Preheat the broiler in your oven.

Toast the slices of white bread until they are golden brown.
Place the toasted bread slices on a baking sheet. Top each slice with slices of roasted turkey.
Pour the Mornay sauce over the turkey on each slice, covering it generously.
Add two slices of cooked bacon on top of the Mornay sauce.
Place the baking sheet under the broiler for a few minutes, just until the sauce starts to bubble and turn golden brown.
Remove from the oven and place slices of tomato on top of each Hot Brown.
Garnish with a sprinkle of paprika and chopped fresh parsley.

Serve the Kentucky Hot Brown immediately while it's warm. It's a rich and indulgent dish, perfect for a comforting meal!

Tennessee Hot Chicken

Ingredients:

For the Chicken:

- 4-6 chicken quarters (legs and thighs)
- 1 cup buttermilk
- 2 cups all-purpose flour
- 1 tablespoon salt
- 1 tablespoon black pepper
- 1 tablespoon smoked paprika
- 1 teaspoon cayenne pepper (adjust to taste)
- Vegetable oil for frying

For the Hot Sauce:

- 1/2 cup hot sauce (such as cayenne pepper-based hot sauce)
- 1/2 cup unsalted butter
- 1 tablespoon brown sugar
- 1 teaspoon paprika
- 1 teaspoon garlic powder
- 1 teaspoon onion powder
- 1/2 teaspoon cayenne pepper (adjust to taste)
- Salt to taste

Instructions:

For the Chicken:

In a large bowl, marinate the chicken quarters in buttermilk for at least 2 hours or overnight in the refrigerator.
In a separate bowl, mix together flour, salt, black pepper, smoked paprika, and cayenne pepper to create the coating mixture.
Preheat the oven to 400°F (200°C).
Heat vegetable oil in a deep fryer or a large, deep skillet to 350°F (175°C).

Dredge each marinated chicken quarter in the flour mixture, ensuring they are well coated.

Fry the chicken in batches until golden brown and crispy, about 15-20 minutes. Ensure the internal temperature reaches 165°F (74°C).

Place the fried chicken on a wire rack to drain excess oil.

For the Hot Sauce:

In a saucepan, melt the butter over low heat. Add hot sauce, brown sugar, paprika, garlic powder, onion powder, cayenne pepper, and salt.

Stir the hot sauce mixture until well combined and heated through. Taste and adjust the spice level and salt as needed.

Assembly:

Dip each piece of fried chicken into the hot sauce mixture, ensuring they are well coated.

Place the hot chicken on a baking sheet lined with parchment paper.

Bake in the preheated oven for about 10 minutes to set the hot sauce and crisp up the chicken.

Serve the Tennessee Hot Chicken with pickles, white bread, and coleslaw for a classic Southern experience. Adjust the heat level to your liking and enjoy this spicy and flavorful dish!

Side Dishes:

Collard Greens with Ham Hocks

Ingredients:

- 2 bunches of collard greens, stems removed and leaves chopped
- 2 smoked ham hocks
- 1 large onion, finely chopped
- 3 cloves garlic, minced
- 4 cups chicken broth
- 1 teaspoon red pepper flakes (optional, for heat)
- Salt and black pepper to taste
- 2 tablespoons apple cider vinegar
- 1 tablespoon brown sugar (optional, for sweetness)
- 2 tablespoons vegetable oil

Instructions:

Prepare the Ham Hocks:
- Rinse the smoked ham hocks under cold water. Place them in a large pot.

Saute Onions and Garlic:
- Heat vegetable oil in the pot over medium heat. Add chopped onions and minced garlic. Saute until the onions are translucent.

Add Ham Hocks and Broth:
- Place the ham hocks back in the pot. Pour in the chicken broth until the ham hocks are mostly covered. Bring the broth to a simmer.

Simmer the Ham Hocks:
- Reduce the heat to low, cover the pot, and let the ham hocks simmer for about 1 to 1.5 hours or until they are tender and the meat is pulling away from the bones.

Prepare Collard Greens:
- While the ham hocks are simmering, wash the collard greens thoroughly. Remove the tough stems and chop the leaves into bite-sized pieces.

Cook Collard Greens:
- Add the collard greens to the pot with the ham hocks.
- Season with red pepper flakes (if using), salt, and black pepper. Stir well.

Simmer Collard Greens:

- Cover the pot and let the collard greens simmer in the flavorful broth for about 45 minutes to 1 hour or until they are tender.

Finish and Serve:
- Once the collard greens are tender, add apple cider vinegar and brown sugar (if using) to balance the flavors. Adjust the seasoning to your liking.

Serve:
- Serve the Collard Greens with Ham Hocks hot, along with the tender ham hocks. You can serve them with cornbread or rice.

Enjoy this comforting and soulful dish of Collard Greens with Ham Hocks!

Southern Corn Pudding

Ingredients:

- 4 cups frozen or fresh corn kernels
- 1/2 cup unsalted butter, melted
- 3 large eggs, beaten
- 1 cup sour cream
- 1 cup whole milk
- 1/2 cup cornmeal
- 1/4 cup all-purpose flour
- 1/4 cup sugar
- 1 teaspoon baking powder
- 1 teaspoon salt
- 1/4 teaspoon black pepper
- Chopped fresh parsley for garnish (optional)

Instructions:

Preheat your oven to 350°F (175°C). Grease a baking dish (9x13 inches or a similar size) with butter or non-stick cooking spray.

In a large mixing bowl, combine the melted butter, beaten eggs, sour cream, and whole milk. Mix well.

In a separate bowl, whisk together the cornmeal, flour, sugar, baking powder, salt, and black pepper.

Gradually add the dry ingredients to the wet ingredients, stirring until well combined and smooth.

Fold in the corn kernels until evenly distributed in the batter.

Pour the corn pudding mixture into the prepared baking dish.

Bake in the preheated oven for approximately 45-50 minutes or until the top is golden brown and the pudding is set in the center.

Allow the corn pudding to cool for a few minutes before serving.

Optionally, garnish with chopped fresh parsley for a burst of color.

Serve the Southern Corn Pudding as a delightful side dish with your favorite Southern meals. It's a comforting and rich addition to any feast!

Baked Macaroni and Cheese

Ingredients:

- 8 oz (about 2 cups) elbow macaroni
- 1/4 cup unsalted butter
- 1/4 cup all-purpose flour
- 1/2 teaspoon salt
- 1/4 teaspoon black pepper
- 1/4 teaspoon dry mustard powder
- 1/4 teaspoon onion powder
- 1/4 teaspoon garlic powder
- 2 1/2 cups milk (whole milk works best)
- 2 1/2 cups shredded sharp cheddar cheese
- 1/2 cup grated Parmesan cheese
- 1/2 cup breadcrumbs (optional, for topping)

Instructions:

Preheat Oven:
- Preheat your oven to 350°F (175°C).

Cook the Macaroni:
- Cook the elbow macaroni according to the package instructions. Drain and set aside.

Make the Cheese Sauce:
- In a large saucepan, melt the butter over medium heat. Stir in the flour, salt, black pepper, mustard powder, onion powder, and garlic powder. Cook, stirring constantly, for 1-2 minutes to create a roux.
- Gradually whisk in the milk to the roux, making sure to eliminate any lumps. Continue cooking and stirring until the mixture thickens, about 5-7 minutes.
- Reduce the heat to low, and stir in the shredded cheddar cheese and grated Parmesan cheese. Keep stirring until the cheese is fully melted and the sauce is smooth.

Combine Sauce and Macaroni:
- Add the cooked macaroni to the cheese sauce, stirring until all the macaroni is well coated.

Bake:
- Transfer the macaroni and cheese mixture to a greased baking dish.

- Optionally, sprinkle breadcrumbs evenly over the top for a crispy crust.
- Bake in the preheated oven for about 25-30 minutes or until the top is golden brown and the edges are bubbling.

Serve:
- Let it cool for a few minutes before serving. This allows the cheese to set a bit.
- Serve the Baked Macaroni and Cheese hot, and enjoy its gooey, cheesy goodness!

Feel free to customize this recipe by adding extra ingredients like cooked bacon, diced tomatoes, or breadcrumbs for additional texture and flavor.

Fried Okra

Ingredients:

- 1 pound fresh okra, sliced into 1/2-inch rounds
- 1 cup buttermilk
- 1 cup cornmeal
- 1/2 cup all-purpose flour
- 1 teaspoon salt
- 1/2 teaspoon black pepper
- 1/4 teaspoon cayenne pepper (optional, for heat)
- Vegetable oil for frying

Instructions:

Prepare the Okra:
- Wash the okra and trim the ends. Cut the okra into 1/2-inch rounds.

Soak in Buttermilk:
- Place the sliced okra in a bowl and pour buttermilk over it. Allow it to soak for at least 30 minutes, or even overnight in the refrigerator. This helps reduce the sliminess of the okra.

Prepare the Coating Mixture:
- In a separate bowl, combine cornmeal, all-purpose flour, salt, black pepper, and cayenne pepper (if using).

Coat the Okra:
- Heat vegetable oil in a deep skillet or fryer to 350°F (175°C).
- Take each slice of okra from the buttermilk, letting excess liquid drip off, and dredge it in the cornmeal mixture until well coated. Shake off any excess coating.

Fry the Okra:
- Carefully place the coated okra slices into the hot oil, working in batches to avoid overcrowding. Fry until golden brown, about 3-4 minutes per batch.
- Use a slotted spoon or tongs to transfer the fried okra to a paper towel-lined plate to drain excess oil.

Serve:
- Serve the Fried Okra hot as a side dish or snack.

Enjoy the crispy goodness of Fried Okra with its distinct Southern flavor. It pairs well with a dipping sauce like ranch dressing or aioli.

Candied Sweet Potatoes

Ingredients:

- 4-5 medium-sized sweet potatoes, peeled and sliced into rounds
- 1/2 cup unsalted butter, melted
- 1 cup brown sugar, packed
- 1/2 teaspoon ground cinnamon
- 1/4 teaspoon ground nutmeg
- 1/4 teaspoon salt
- 1 teaspoon vanilla extract
- 1/2 cup water
- Chopped pecans or marshmallows (optional, for topping)

Instructions:

Preheat Oven:
- Preheat your oven to 375°F (190°C).

Prepare Sweet Potatoes:
- Peel the sweet potatoes and slice them into rounds, about 1/4 to 1/2 inch thick.

Make the Candied Sauce:
- In a mixing bowl, combine melted butter, brown sugar, ground cinnamon, ground nutmeg, salt, and vanilla extract. Mix until well combined.

Coat Sweet Potatoes:
- Place the sliced sweet potatoes in a baking dish. Pour the candied sauce over the sweet potatoes, making sure they are well coated.

Add Water:
- Pour water into the baking dish around the sweet potatoes. This helps create steam, making the sweet potatoes tender as they bake.

Bake:
- Cover the baking dish with aluminum foil and bake in the preheated oven for about 30 minutes.
- After 30 minutes, remove the foil and continue baking for an additional 15-20 minutes or until the sweet potatoes are tender and the sauce has thickened.

Optional Toppings:
- If desired, during the last 5-10 minutes of baking, you can add chopped pecans or marshmallows on top for a crunchy or gooey finish.

Serve:
- Once baked, let the candied sweet potatoes cool for a few minutes before serving.

Candied sweet potatoes make a delightful side dish for any occasion, and they are particularly popular during Thanksgiving and other holiday meals. Enjoy the sweet and spiced flavor of this Southern classic!

Creamed Corn

Ingredients:

- 4 cups fresh or frozen corn kernels (about 6-8 ears of corn)
- 1/4 cup unsalted butter
- 1/4 cup all-purpose flour
- 2 cups whole milk
- 2 tablespoons sugar
- Salt and black pepper to taste
- Optional: 1/4 cup heavy cream for extra richness
- Optional: Chopped fresh parsley or chives for garnish

Instructions:

Prepare the Corn:
- If using fresh corn, cut the kernels from the cob. If using frozen corn, thaw it according to the package instructions.

Make the Roux:
- In a large skillet or saucepan, melt the butter over medium heat. Add the flour and whisk continuously to create a roux. Cook for 2-3 minutes until the roux is lightly golden.

Add Milk:
- Gradually pour in the milk, whisking constantly to avoid lumps. Continue to whisk until the mixture thickens.

Combine Corn:
- Add the corn kernels to the skillet, stirring to combine with the roux and milk mixture.

Season:
- Stir in the sugar and season with salt and black pepper to taste. If you prefer a richer dish, you can also add 1/4 cup of heavy cream at this stage.

Simmer:
- Reduce the heat to low and let the creamed corn simmer for 10-15 minutes, stirring occasionally, until the corn is tender and the flavors have melded.

Adjust Consistency:
- If the creamed corn is too thick, you can add a little more milk to achieve your desired consistency.

Serve:
- Once the creamed corn is cooked to your liking, remove it from heat. Garnish with chopped fresh parsley or chives if desired.

Serve the creamed corn as a side dish, and enjoy the comforting blend of sweetness and creaminess that makes this dish a Southern favorite.

Red Beans and Rice

Ingredients:

- 1 pound dried red kidney beans
- 1 pound andouille sausage, sliced
- 1 large onion, diced
- 1 bell pepper, diced
- 2 celery stalks, diced
- 4 cloves garlic, minced
- 2 bay leaves
- 1 teaspoon dried thyme
- 1 teaspoon dried oregano
- 1 teaspoon smoked paprika
- 1/2 teaspoon cayenne pepper (adjust to taste)
- Salt and black pepper to taste
- 1 ham hock or smoked pork sausage (optional, for extra flavor)
- 6 cups chicken broth or water
- 3 cups cooked white rice
- Green onions for garnish
- Hot sauce for serving (optional)

Instructions:

Prepare the Beans:
- Rinse the dried red kidney beans under cold water. In a large bowl, cover the beans with water and soak them overnight. Alternatively, you can use the quick soak method by bringing the beans to a boil for 2 minutes, then letting them soak for 1 hour.

Saute Sausage and Vegetables:
- In a large pot or Dutch oven, sauté the sliced andouille sausage until browned. Add diced onion, bell pepper, celery, and minced garlic. Cook until the vegetables are softened.

Add Seasonings:
- Stir in bay leaves, dried thyme, dried oregano, smoked paprika, cayenne pepper, salt, and black pepper. Mix well to combine the flavors.

Add Beans and Liquid:

- Drain the soaked beans and add them to the pot. Pour in chicken broth or water. Add a ham hock or smoked pork sausage for additional flavor if using.

Simmer:
- Bring the mixture to a boil, then reduce the heat to low. Cover and simmer for 2-3 hours or until the beans are tender. Stir occasionally, and add more liquid if needed.

Mash Beans (Optional):
- If you prefer a creamier consistency, you can mash some of the beans against the side of the pot with a spoon.

Adjust Seasoning:
- Taste and adjust the seasoning as needed. Remove the bay leaves and any bones from the ham hock.

Serve:
- Serve the red beans over a bed of cooked white rice. Garnish with chopped green onions and offer hot sauce on the side if desired.

Red Beans and Rice is a filling and satisfying dish that captures the essence of Southern comfort food. Enjoy!

Breads:

Buttermilk Biscuits

Ingredients:

- 2 cups all-purpose flour
- 1 tablespoon baking powder
- 1/2 teaspoon baking soda
- 1 teaspoon salt
- 1/2 cup unsalted butter, cold and cut into small pieces
- 1 cup buttermilk, cold
- Extra flour for dusting

Instructions:

Preheat Oven:
- Preheat your oven to 450°F (230°C).

Prepare Baking Sheet:
- Line a baking sheet with parchment paper.

Mix Dry Ingredients:
- In a large mixing bowl, whisk together the all-purpose flour, baking powder, baking soda, and salt.

Cut in Butter:
- Add the cold, diced butter to the flour mixture. Using a pastry cutter or your fingers, cut the butter into the flour until the mixture resembles coarse crumbs.

Add Buttermilk:
- Make a well in the center of the flour mixture and pour in the cold buttermilk. Stir gently with a wooden spoon or your hands until just combined. The dough will be sticky.

Knead the Dough:
- Turn the dough out onto a floured surface. Gently knead it a few times, folding it over itself. Be careful not to overwork the dough; it should still be somewhat sticky.

Roll and Cut:

- Roll out the dough to about 1/2-inch thickness. Using a floured biscuit cutter or a glass, cut out biscuits and place them on the prepared baking sheet. Press straight down without twisting to ensure proper rising.

Bake:
- Bake in the preheated oven for 10-12 minutes or until the biscuits are golden brown on top.

Serve:
- Allow the biscuits to cool for a few minutes before serving. Enjoy them warm with butter, jam, gravy, or your favorite topping.

These buttermilk biscuits are delicious as a side for breakfast, brunch, or dinner. The key to flaky biscuits is handling the dough gently and not overworking it. Enjoy the homemade goodness!

Southern Cornbread

Ingredients:

- 1 cup cornmeal
- 1 cup all-purpose flour
- 1 tablespoon baking powder
- 1 teaspoon salt
- 1 cup buttermilk
- 2 large eggs
- 1/2 cup unsalted butter, melted
- 1 tablespoon vegetable oil (for greasing the pan)

Instructions:

Preheat Oven:
- Preheat your oven to 425°F (220°C). Place a 10-inch cast-iron skillet in the oven while it preheats.

Mix Dry Ingredients:
- In a mixing bowl, whisk together the cornmeal, all-purpose flour, baking powder, and salt.

Prepare Wet Ingredients:
- In a separate bowl, whisk together the buttermilk and eggs until well combined.

Combine Wet and Dry Ingredients:
- Pour the wet ingredients into the bowl with the dry ingredients. Stir until just combined.

Add Melted Butter:
- Pour in the melted butter and stir until the batter is smooth.

Grease Skillet:
- Carefully remove the hot skillet from the oven. Add the vegetable oil to the skillet, swirling it to coat the bottom and sides.

Pour Batter into Skillet:
- Pour the cornbread batter into the hot, greased skillet.

Bake:
- Bake in the preheated oven for 20-25 minutes or until the top is golden brown and a toothpick inserted into the center comes out clean.

Cool and Serve:
- Allow the cornbread to cool for a few minutes before slicing and serving.

Southern cornbread is delicious served warm with butter, honey, or alongside savory dishes like chili, greens, or barbecue. It can also be crumbled into cornbread dressing or used as a base for dishes like cornbread stuffing. Enjoy the authentic flavor of this Southern classic!

Hoppin' John Cornbread

Ingredients:

For the Hoppin' John Filling:

- 1 cup cooked black-eyed peas (canned or cooked from dried)
- 1 cup cooked rice
- 1/2 cup diced ham or bacon (cooked)
- 1/2 cup diced onion
- 1/4 cup diced bell pepper (any color)
- 1/4 cup diced celery
- 2 cloves garlic, minced
- 1 teaspoon dried thyme
- Salt and black pepper to taste
- 1 tablespoon vegetable oil for sautéing

For the Cornbread Batter:

- 1 cup cornmeal
- 1 cup all-purpose flour
- 1 tablespoon baking powder
- 1/2 teaspoon baking soda
- 1 teaspoon salt
- 1 cup buttermilk
- 2 large eggs
- 1/2 cup unsalted butter, melted
- 1 tablespoon honey (optional, for a touch of sweetness)
- 1 cup shredded sharp cheddar cheese (optional)
- 1/4 cup chopped green onions (optional, for garnish)

Instructions:

For the Hoppin' John Filling:

In a skillet, heat the vegetable oil over medium heat. Add diced ham or bacon and sauté until browned.

Add diced onion, bell pepper, celery, and garlic to the skillet. Cook until the vegetables are softened.

Stir in the cooked black-eyed peas and rice. Add dried thyme, salt, and black pepper. Mix well and let the mixture cook for a few minutes. Remove from heat and set aside.

For the Cornbread Batter:

Preheat your oven to 425°F (220°C).

In a large mixing bowl, whisk together cornmeal, all-purpose flour, baking powder, baking soda, and salt.

In another bowl, whisk together buttermilk, eggs, melted butter, and honey (if using).

Pour the wet ingredients into the bowl with the dry ingredients. Stir until just combined. If desired, fold in shredded cheddar cheese.

Assembling Hoppin' John Cornbread:

Grease a baking dish or a cast-iron skillet.

Pour half of the cornbread batter into the prepared dish.

Spoon the Hoppin' John filling evenly over the cornbread batter.

Top with the remaining cornbread batter, spreading it to cover the filling.

Bake in the preheated oven for 20-25 minutes or until the top is golden brown and a toothpick inserted into the center comes out clean.

Optional: Garnish with chopped green onions before serving.

Allow the Hoppin' John Cornbread to cool for a few minutes before slicing and serving.

This dish combines the rich, savory flavors of Hoppin' John with the comforting appeal of cornbread for a unique and delicious experience. Enjoy!

Sweet Potato Biscuits

Ingredients:

- 1 cup cooked and mashed sweet potatoes (about 2 medium-sized sweet potatoes)
- 1/2 cup unsalted butter, cold and cut into small pieces
- 2 1/2 cups all-purpose flour
- 1 tablespoon baking powder
- 1/2 teaspoon baking soda
- 1/2 teaspoon salt
- 1 tablespoon brown sugar
- 3/4 cup buttermilk, cold
- Additional flour for dusting

Instructions:

Prepare Sweet Potatoes:
- Peel, chop, and boil the sweet potatoes until they are fork-tender. Mash them and let them cool to room temperature.

Preheat Oven:
- Preheat your oven to 425°F (220°C).

Cut in Butter:
- In a large mixing bowl, combine the flour, baking powder, baking soda, salt, and brown sugar. Add the cold, diced butter to the dry ingredients. Use a pastry cutter or your fingers to cut the butter into the flour until the mixture resembles coarse crumbs.

Add Sweet Potatoes and Buttermilk:
- Add the mashed sweet potatoes to the flour mixture. Pour in the cold buttermilk. Stir until just combined. The dough should be soft but not overly sticky.

Knead and Roll:
- Turn the dough out onto a floured surface. Gently knead it a few times, then roll it out to about 1/2-inch thickness.

Cut Biscuits:
- Use a floured biscuit cutter or a glass to cut out biscuits from the rolled dough. Place the biscuits on a baking sheet lined with parchment paper.

Bake:

- Bake in the preheated oven for 12-15 minutes or until the biscuits are golden brown on top.

Serve:
- Allow the sweet potato biscuits to cool for a few minutes before serving. Serve them warm with butter or your favorite topping.

These Sweet Potato Biscuits offer a unique twist with a subtle sweetness and a lovely orange hue from the sweet potatoes. They are a perfect side for breakfast, brunch, or as an accompaniment to your favorite Southern dishes. Enjoy!

Parker House Rolls

Ingredients:

- 4 cups all-purpose flour
- 1/4 cup granulated sugar
- 1 teaspoon salt
- 1 packet (2 1/4 teaspoons) active dry yeast
- 1 1/2 cups warm milk (about 110°F or 43°C)
- 1/2 cup unsalted butter, melted (plus additional for brushing)
- 1 large egg

Instructions:

Activate Yeast:
- In a small bowl, combine warm milk and a pinch of sugar. Sprinkle the yeast over the milk and let it sit for 5-10 minutes until it becomes frothy.

Mix Dry Ingredients:
- In a large mixing bowl, whisk together the flour, sugar, and salt.

Combine Wet Ingredients:
- In another bowl, whisk together the melted butter and the egg.

Make Dough:
- Add the activated yeast mixture to the dry ingredients, followed by the butter and egg mixture. Stir until a soft dough forms.

Knead Dough:
- Turn the dough out onto a floured surface and knead for about 5-7 minutes until smooth and elastic.

First Rise:
- Place the dough in a lightly greased bowl, cover it with a clean kitchen towel, and let it rise in a warm place for 1-1.5 hours, or until doubled in size.

Shape Rolls:
- Preheat your oven to 375°F (190°C). Punch down the risen dough and turn it out onto a floured surface. Roll it into a rectangle about 1/2-inch thick.
- Using a round biscuit or cookie cutter, cut out rounds from the dough. Optionally, you can use a knife to cut the dough into squares.

Fold Rolls:
- Brush each round with melted butter, and if desired, fold the round in half to create a half-moon shape (traditional for Parker House Rolls).

Second Rise:
- Place the shaped rolls on a baking sheet lined with parchment paper. Cover with a towel and let them rise for another 30-45 minutes.

Bake:
- Bake in the preheated oven for 15-20 minutes or until the rolls are golden brown.

Brush with Butter:
- As soon as the rolls come out of the oven, brush the tops with additional melted butter.

Serve:
- Allow the Parker House Rolls to cool for a few minutes before serving.

These buttery, soft, and slightly sweet rolls are a classic addition to any meal. Serve them warm with dinner or use them as slider buns for sandwiches. Enjoy!

Salads:

Southern Cobb Salad

Ingredients:

For the Salad:

- 4 cups mixed salad greens (lettuce, spinach, or your choice)
- 1 cup cooked and diced chicken (seasoned with Southern spices if desired)
- 1 cup cherry tomatoes, halved
- 1 cup corn kernels (fresh, frozen, or canned)
- 1 cup black-eyed peas, cooked (canned or cooked from dried)
- 1 avocado, diced
- 4 slices bacon, cooked and crumbled
- 1/2 cup crumbled feta or blue cheese
- Hard-boiled eggs, sliced

For the Dressing:

- 1/4 cup olive oil
- 2 tablespoons apple cider vinegar
- 1 tablespoon Dijon mustard
- 1 teaspoon honey
- Salt and black pepper to taste
- 1 teaspoon Southern seasoning blend (optional)

Instructions:

Prepare Salad Ingredients:
- Cook and dice the chicken, cook the bacon until crispy, hard-boil the eggs, and prepare other salad ingredients.

Assemble Salad:
- Arrange the mixed salad greens on a large serving platter or in individual bowls.
- Arrange the cooked and diced chicken, cherry tomatoes, corn, black-eyed peas, diced avocado, crumbled bacon, crumbled cheese, and sliced hard-boiled eggs on top of the greens in rows or sections.

Make the Dressing:

- In a small bowl, whisk together olive oil, apple cider vinegar, Dijon mustard, honey, salt, black pepper, and the optional Southern seasoning blend. Adjust the seasoning to your taste.

Serve:
- Drizzle the dressing over the Southern Cobb Salad just before serving.

Optional Garnish:
- Garnish with additional crumbled cheese, bacon, and chopped green onions if desired.

Enjoy:
- Toss the salad gently or let individuals mix their own salads at the table. Enjoy this Southern Cobb Salad as a flavorful and hearty meal.

Feel free to customize the salad with your favorite Southern ingredients and dressing variations. It's a refreshing and satisfying dish that captures the essence of Southern flavors.

Classic Potato Salad

Ingredients:

- 2 pounds (about 4 cups) russet potatoes, peeled and diced into 1/2-inch cubes
- 3 large eggs, hard-boiled and chopped
- 1/2 cup celery, finely chopped
- 1/4 cup red onion, finely chopped
- 1/4 cup dill pickles, finely chopped
- 1/2 cup mayonnaise
- 2 tablespoons Dijon mustard
- 1 tablespoon apple cider vinegar
- Salt and black pepper to taste
- Paprika for garnish (optional)
- Fresh parsley, chopped, for garnish (optional)

Instructions:

Boil Potatoes:
- Place the diced potatoes in a large pot of cold, salted water. Bring to a boil and cook until the potatoes are fork-tender but still firm, about 8-10 minutes. Be careful not to overcook. Drain and let the potatoes cool.

Prepare Eggs:
- Hard-boil the eggs, let them cool, and then chop them into small pieces.

Combine Ingredients:
- In a large mixing bowl, combine the cooled diced potatoes, chopped hard-boiled eggs, celery, red onion, and dill pickles.

Make Dressing:
- In a small bowl, whisk together mayonnaise, Dijon mustard, apple cider vinegar, salt, and black pepper.

Combine Salad:
- Pour the dressing over the potato mixture and gently toss until everything is well coated.

Chill:
- Cover the potato salad and refrigerate for at least 1-2 hours to allow the flavors to meld and the salad to chill.

Serve:
- Before serving, check the seasoning and adjust if necessary. Sprinkle with paprika for color and garnish with chopped fresh parsley if desired.

Enjoy:
- Serve the Classic Potato Salad as a side dish for picnics, barbecues, or alongside your favorite main courses.

This Classic Potato Salad is simple, creamy, and full of flavor. It's a timeless recipe that's sure to be a hit at any gathering.

Fried Green Tomato Salad

Ingredients:

For the Fried Green Tomatoes:

- 4 large green tomatoes, sliced into 1/2-inch rounds
- 1 cup buttermilk
- 1 cup cornmeal
- 1 cup all-purpose flour
- 1 teaspoon salt
- 1/2 teaspoon black pepper
- Vegetable oil for frying

For the Salad:

- Mixed salad greens (lettuce, arugula, or your choice)
- Cherry tomatoes, halved
- Red onion, thinly sliced
- Feta cheese, crumbled
- Balsamic vinaigrette dressing

Instructions:

For the Fried Green Tomatoes:

Prepare Tomatoes:
- Slice the green tomatoes into 1/2-inch rounds.

Soak in Buttermilk:
- Place the tomato slices in a shallow dish and pour buttermilk over them. Let them soak for at least 30 minutes.

Prepare Coating:
- In a separate bowl, combine cornmeal, all-purpose flour, salt, and black pepper.

Coat Tomatoes:
- Heat vegetable oil in a skillet or frying pan over medium-high heat.
- Take each soaked tomato slice, letting excess buttermilk drip off, and dredge it in the cornmeal mixture until well coated. Shake off any excess coating.

Fry Tomatoes:

- Carefully place the coated tomato slices into the hot oil. Fry until golden brown on both sides, about 3-4 minutes per side. Transfer to a paper towel-lined plate to drain excess oil.

For the Salad:
- Arrange mixed salad greens on a serving platter or individual plates.
- Top the greens with fried green tomato slices, halved cherry tomatoes, thinly sliced red onion, and crumbled feta cheese.

Dress the Salad:
- Drizzle the salad with balsamic vinaigrette dressing just before serving.

Serve:
- Serve the Fried Green Tomato Salad immediately while the tomatoes are still warm.

This salad combines the crispy texture of fried green tomatoes with the freshness of salad greens, creating a delightful contrast of flavors and textures. Enjoy the unique and Southern-inspired Fried Green Tomato Salad!

Watermelon and Feta Salad

Ingredients:

- 4 cups seedless watermelon, cubed
- 1 cup feta cheese, crumbled
- 1 cup cucumber, diced
- 1/4 cup red onion, thinly sliced
- 1/4 cup fresh mint leaves, chopped
- 2 tablespoons extra-virgin olive oil
- 1 tablespoon balsamic vinegar
- Salt and black pepper to taste

Instructions:

Prepare Ingredients:
- Cut the watermelon into bite-sized cubes. If using cucumber with seeds, you may want to scoop out the seeds before dicing.

Assemble Salad:
- In a large salad bowl, combine the watermelon cubes, crumbled feta cheese, diced cucumber, sliced red onion, and chopped mint leaves.

Make Dressing:
- In a small bowl, whisk together the extra-virgin olive oil and balsamic vinegar. Season with salt and black pepper to taste.

Dress Salad:
- Drizzle the dressing over the watermelon and feta mixture. Gently toss the salad until all ingredients are well coated.

Chill (Optional):
- If desired, you can refrigerate the salad for about 30 minutes to allow the flavors to meld and the salad to chill.

Serve:
- Serve the Watermelon and Feta Salad in bowls or on a platter.

This salad is a delightful combination of sweet, salty, and savory flavors with a burst of freshness from the mint. It's perfect for hot summer days or as a refreshing side dish for a variety of meals. Enjoy!

Shrimp Remoulade Salad

Ingredients:

For the Shrimp:

- 1 pound large shrimp, peeled and deveined
- 1 tablespoon olive oil
- 1 teaspoon Cajun seasoning
- Salt and black pepper to taste
- Lemon wedges for garnish

For the Remoulade Sauce:

- 1 cup mayonnaise
- 2 tablespoons Dijon mustard
- 1 tablespoon whole grain mustard
- 1 tablespoon ketchup
- 1 tablespoon hot sauce (adjust to taste)
- 1 tablespoon Worcestershire sauce
- 2 green onions, finely chopped
- 2 cloves garlic, minced
- 1 tablespoon capers, chopped
- 1 tablespoon fresh parsley, chopped
- Salt and black pepper to taste

For the Salad:

- Mixed salad greens
- Cherry tomatoes, halved
- Cucumber, sliced
- Avocado, sliced
- Lemon wedges for garnish

Instructions:

For the Shrimp:

Season Shrimp:
- In a bowl, toss the shrimp with olive oil, Cajun seasoning, salt, and black pepper until well coated.

Cook Shrimp:
- Heat a skillet or grill pan over medium-high heat. Cook the shrimp for 2-3 minutes per side or until they are pink and opaque. Remove from heat.

For the Remoulade Sauce:

Make Remoulade Sauce:
- In a bowl, whisk together mayonnaise, Dijon mustard, whole grain mustard, ketchup, hot sauce, Worcestershire sauce, green onions, garlic, capers, parsley, salt, and black pepper. Adjust the seasoning to taste.

Assemble Shrimp Remoulade Salad:

Prepare Salad:
- In a large serving bowl or individual plates, arrange mixed salad greens, cherry tomatoes, cucumber slices, and avocado slices.

Add Shrimp:
- Place the cooked shrimp on top of the salad.

Drizzle with Remoulade Sauce:
- Drizzle the prepared remoulade sauce over the shrimp and salad.

Garnish:
- Garnish with lemon wedges.

Serve:
- Serve the Shrimp Remoulade Salad immediately, allowing diners to squeeze fresh lemon juice over their salads if desired.

This Shrimp Remoulade Salad is a wonderful combination of bold flavors and textures, making it a perfect choice for a light and satisfying meal. Enjoy!

Casseroles:

Chicken and Rice Casserole

Ingredients:

- 1.5 to 2 pounds boneless, skinless chicken breasts or thighs, cut into bite-sized pieces
- 1 cup long-grain white rice
- 2 cups chicken broth
- 1 cup frozen peas and carrots mix
- 1 medium onion, finely chopped
- 2 cloves garlic, minced
- 1 teaspoon dried thyme
- 1 teaspoon dried rosemary
- 1/2 teaspoon dried sage
- Salt and black pepper to taste
- 1 cup shredded cheddar cheese
- 1/2 cup grated Parmesan cheese
- 1 cup milk
- 2 tablespoons all-purpose flour
- 2 tablespoons butter
- Chopped fresh parsley for garnish (optional)

Instructions:

Preheat Oven:
- Preheat your oven to 375°F (190°C).

Cook Chicken:
- Season the chicken pieces with salt and black pepper. In a large skillet, cook the chicken over medium-high heat until browned on all sides. Remove from the skillet and set aside.

Saute Onion and Garlic:
- In the same skillet, add a bit of oil if needed and sauté the chopped onion until translucent. Add minced garlic and sauté for an additional minute.

Prepare Rice:
- Add the rice to the skillet and cook for a couple of minutes, stirring to coat the rice with the onion and garlic mixture.

Add Herbs and Vegetables:
- Stir in the dried thyme, rosemary, sage, frozen peas, and carrots mix.

Combine Chicken and Rice Mixture:
- Return the cooked chicken to the skillet, mixing it with the rice and vegetables.

Make Cheese Sauce:
- In a separate saucepan, melt the butter over medium heat. Stir in the flour to create a roux. Gradually whisk in the milk until the mixture thickens. Add the shredded cheddar and Parmesan cheese, stirring until melted and smooth.

Combine Cheese Sauce with Chicken and Rice:
- Pour the cheese sauce over the chicken and rice mixture, stirring to coat evenly.

Transfer to Casserole Dish:
- Transfer the mixture to a greased casserole dish.

Bake:
- Cover the casserole dish with foil and bake in the preheated oven for about 30 minutes. Remove the foil and continue baking for an additional 10-15 minutes or until the top is golden brown and the casserole is bubbly.

Garnish and Serve:
- Garnish with chopped fresh parsley if desired. Serve the Chicken and Rice Casserole hot.

This Chicken and Rice Casserole is a satisfying and complete meal that the whole family will enjoy. Feel free to customize it by adding your favorite vegetables or using different herbs and spices. Enjoy!

Grits Casserole

Ingredients:

- 1 cup stone-ground grits
- 4 cups water
- 1 teaspoon salt
- 1 cup milk
- 1/2 cup unsalted butter
- 2 cups shredded sharp cheddar cheese
- 4 large eggs, beaten
- 1/4 teaspoon black pepper
- 1/4 teaspoon cayenne pepper (optional for a bit of heat)
- 1/2 cup green onions, finely chopped
- 1/2 cup cooked and crumbled bacon or sausage (optional for additional flavor)
- Cooking spray or additional butter for greasing the casserole dish

Instructions:

Preheat Oven:
- Preheat your oven to 350°F (175°C).

Cook Grits:
- In a medium saucepan, bring 4 cups of water to a boil. Gradually whisk in the grits and salt. Reduce the heat to low, cover, and simmer for about 20-25 minutes or until the grits are thick and creamy, stirring occasionally.

Add Milk and Butter:
- Stir in the milk, butter, and shredded cheddar cheese until the cheese is melted and the mixture is smooth.

Temper Eggs:
- In a separate bowl, beat the eggs. To prevent the eggs from curdling when added to the hot grits, gradually whisk in a small amount of the hot grits mixture into the beaten eggs to temper them.

Combine Grits and Eggs:
- Pour the tempered eggs into the grits mixture, stirring continuously to combine.

Season and Add Extras:
- Season the grits with black pepper and cayenne pepper (if using). Stir in chopped green onions and cooked, crumbled bacon or sausage if desired.

Grease Casserole Dish:
- Grease a baking dish or casserole dish with cooking spray or butter.

Pour Mixture into Dish:
- Pour the grits mixture into the prepared casserole dish, spreading it evenly.

Bake:
- Bake in the preheated oven for 40-45 minutes or until the casserole is set and the top is golden brown.

Serve:
- Allow the Grits Casserole to cool for a few minutes before serving. Slice and serve warm.

This Grits Casserole is a comforting and versatile dish that pairs well with a variety of main courses or can stand alone as a delicious side dish. Feel free to customize it by adding your favorite ingredients like sautéed vegetables or different types of cheese. Enjoy!

Squash Casserole

Ingredients:

- 6 cups yellow squash, sliced
- 1/2 cup onion, finely chopped
- 1/2 cup butter
- 1 cup shredded cheddar cheese
- 2 large eggs, beaten
- 1/2 cup sour cream
- 1/2 cup mayonnaise
- 1 cup breadcrumbs
- Salt and black pepper to taste
- 1/2 teaspoon garlic powder (optional)
- 1/4 cup fresh parsley, chopped (optional, for garnish)

Instructions:

Preheat Oven:
- Preheat your oven to 350°F (175°C).

Boil Squash:
- Place the sliced yellow squash and chopped onion in a large pot. Add enough water to cover the squash. Bring to a boil and cook for about 5 minutes or until the squash is tender. Drain the water.

Saute Squash and Onions:
- In the same pot, melt the butter over medium heat. Add the boiled squash and onions. Cook for an additional 5 minutes, stirring occasionally. Remove from heat.

Prepare Casserole Mixture:
- In a large mixing bowl, combine the sautéed squash and onions with shredded cheddar cheese, beaten eggs, sour cream, mayonnaise, breadcrumbs, salt, black pepper, and garlic powder (if using). Mix well to combine.

Assemble Casserole:
- Transfer the mixture to a greased baking dish, spreading it evenly.

Bake:
- Bake in the preheated oven for 25-30 minutes or until the top is golden brown and the casserole is set.

Garnish (Optional):

- If desired, garnish the Squash Casserole with chopped fresh parsley before serving.

Serve:
- Allow the casserole to cool for a few minutes before serving. Slice and serve warm.

This Squash Casserole is a wonderful way to enjoy the flavors of fresh summer squash. It makes a great side dish for a variety of meals and is a perfect addition to any Southern-inspired feast. Enjoy!

Baked Chicken and Cornbread Dressing

Ingredients:

For the Chicken:

- 4 boneless, skinless chicken breasts
- Salt and black pepper to taste
- 1 teaspoon paprika
- 1 teaspoon garlic powder
- 1 teaspoon onion powder
- 1 teaspoon dried thyme
- 2 tablespoons olive oil

For the Cornbread Dressing:

- 4 cups crumbled cornbread (pre-baked and cooled)
- 1 cup celery, finely chopped
- 1 cup onion, finely chopped
- 1 cup chicken broth
- 2 eggs, beaten
- 1/2 cup unsalted butter, melted
- 1 teaspoon dried sage
- Salt and black pepper to taste

For the Gravy:

- 2 cups chicken broth
- 1/4 cup all-purpose flour
- Salt and black pepper to taste

Instructions:

For the Chicken:

Preheat Oven:
- Preheat your oven to 375°F (190°C).

Season Chicken:
- Season the chicken breasts with salt, black pepper, paprika, garlic powder, onion powder, and dried thyme.

Sear Chicken:
- Heat olive oil in an oven-safe skillet over medium-high heat. Sear the chicken breasts on both sides until browned.

Bake Chicken:
- Transfer the skillet to the preheated oven and bake for 20-25 minutes or until the chicken reaches an internal temperature of 165°F (74°C). Remove from the oven and let it rest.

For the Cornbread Dressing:

Prepare Cornbread:
- Pre-bake cornbread according to your preferred recipe. Once cooled, crumble it into a large mixing bowl.

Saute Vegetables:
- In a skillet, sauté chopped celery and onion until softened.

Mix Dressing:
- In the bowl with crumbled cornbread, add sautéed vegetables, chicken broth, beaten eggs, melted butter, dried sage, salt, and black pepper. Mix everything well.

Transfer to Baking Dish:
- Transfer the cornbread dressing mixture to a greased baking dish.

Bake Dressing:
- Bake in the preheated oven alongside the chicken for about 25-30 minutes or until the dressing is set and golden brown on top.

For the Gravy:

Make Gravy:
- In a saucepan, whisk together chicken broth and flour. Bring to a simmer, stirring constantly until the gravy thickens. Season with salt and black pepper to taste.

Serve:
- Serve the baked chicken over a generous portion of cornbread dressing, and drizzle with the prepared gravy.

This Baked Chicken and Cornbread Dressing is a hearty and satisfying meal, capturing the essence of Southern comfort food. Enjoy!

Crawfish Étouffée Casserole

Ingredients:

For the Crawfish Étouffée:

- 1/2 cup unsalted butter
- 1/2 cup all-purpose flour
- 1 large onion, finely chopped
- 1 bell pepper, finely chopped
- 2 celery stalks, finely chopped
- 3 cloves garlic, minced
- 1 pound crawfish tails, peeled and deveined
- 1 can (14.5 ounces) diced tomatoes, undrained
- 1 cup chicken or seafood broth
- 1 teaspoon Cajun seasoning
- 1/2 teaspoon paprika
- Salt and black pepper to taste
- Green onions, chopped, for garnish
- Fresh parsley, chopped, for garnish
- Cooked rice, for serving

For the Casserole:

- 4 cups cooked white rice
- 1 cup shredded cheddar cheese
- 1/2 cup sour cream
- 2 large eggs, beaten
- 1/4 cup milk
- Salt and black pepper to taste

Instructions:

For the Crawfish Étouffée:

Make Roux:

- In a large skillet, melt butter over medium heat. Add flour and stir continuously to make a roux. Cook until the roux is a dark golden brown, taking care not to burn it.

Sauté Vegetables:
- Add chopped onion, bell pepper, celery, and minced garlic to the roux. Sauté until the vegetables are softened.

Add Crawfish:
- Add crawfish tails to the skillet and cook for a few minutes until they start to turn opaque.

Season:
- Stir in diced tomatoes (with their juice), chicken or seafood broth, Cajun seasoning, paprika, salt, and black pepper. Simmer for 15-20 minutes, allowing the flavors to meld and the mixture to thicken.

Garnish:
- Garnish with chopped green onions and fresh parsley. Adjust seasoning if needed.

For the Casserole:

Preheat Oven:
- Preheat your oven to 350°F (175°C).

Prepare Casserole Mixture:
- In a large bowl, combine cooked white rice, shredded cheddar cheese, sour cream, beaten eggs, milk, salt, and black pepper.

Layer Casserole:
- In a greased casserole dish, spread half of the rice mixture evenly. Top it with the crawfish étouffée.

Add Remaining Rice Mixture:
- Cover the crawfish étouffée with the remaining rice mixture.

Bake:
- Bake in the preheated oven for 30-35 minutes or until the top is golden brown and the casserole is set.

Serve:
- Allow the Crawfish Étouffée Casserole to cool for a few minutes before serving. Serve over additional rice if desired.

This Crawfish Étouffée Casserole is a flavorful and comforting dish that brings the essence of Cajun cuisine to your table. Enjoy the rich and spicy flavors!

Desserts:

Pecan Pie

Ingredients:

For the Pie Crust:

- 1 1/4 cups all-purpose flour
- 1/2 cup unsalted butter, cold and cut into small cubes
- 1/4 cup granulated sugar
- 1/4 teaspoon salt
- 2-3 tablespoons ice water

For the Pecan Filling:

- 1 cup granulated sugar
- 1 cup corn syrup (light or dark)
- 3 large eggs
- 1/4 cup unsalted butter, melted
- 1 teaspoon vanilla extract
- 1/4 teaspoon salt
- 1 1/2 cups pecan halves

Instructions:

For the Pie Crust:

Prepare Pie Crust:
- In a food processor, combine flour, sugar, and salt. Add cold butter cubes and pulse until the mixture resembles coarse crumbs.

Add Ice Water:
- With the processor running, gradually add ice water until the dough begins to come together. Stop processing once the dough forms into a ball.

Chill Dough:
- Flatten the dough into a disk, wrap it in plastic wrap, and refrigerate for at least 1 hour.

Roll Out Crust:

- On a floured surface, roll out the chilled dough into a circle large enough to fit your pie dish. Transfer the crust to the dish, trim excess, and crimp the edges.

For the Pecan Filling:

Preheat Oven:
- Preheat your oven to 350°F (175°C).

Prepare Pecans:
- Arrange the pecan halves on the bottom of the pie crust.

Make Filling:
- In a mixing bowl, whisk together sugar, corn syrup, eggs, melted butter, vanilla extract, and salt until well combined.

Pour Over Pecans:
- Pour the filling mixture over the arranged pecans in the pie crust.

Bake:
- Bake in the preheated oven for 50-60 minutes or until the center is set and a toothpick inserted comes out clean.

Cool:
- Allow the pecan pie to cool completely before slicing.

Serve:
- Serve the Pecan Pie at room temperature. Optionally, top with whipped cream or a scoop of vanilla ice cream.

This Pecan Pie recipe yields a classic Southern dessert with a perfect balance of sweetness and nuttiness. Enjoy this delicious treat on its own or as part of a festive holiday spread.

Peach Cobbler

Ingredients:

For the Peach Filling:

- 6 cups fresh or canned peach slices (about 6-8 peaches)
- 1 cup granulated sugar
- 1 tablespoon lemon juice
- 1 teaspoon vanilla extract
- 1/4 teaspoon ground cinnamon
- 2 tablespoons cornstarch (for fresh peaches) or 1 tablespoon all-purpose flour (for canned peaches)

For the Cobbler Topping:

- 1 cup all-purpose flour
- 1 cup granulated sugar
- 1 teaspoon baking powder
- 1/2 teaspoon salt
- 1/2 cup unsalted butter, melted
- 3/4 cup milk
- 1 teaspoon vanilla extract

Instructions:

Preheat Oven:
- Preheat your oven to 375°F (190°C).

Prepare Peaches:
- If using fresh peaches, peel, pit, and slice them. In a large bowl, combine the peach slices with sugar, lemon juice, vanilla extract, ground cinnamon, and cornstarch (for fresh peaches) or flour (for canned peaches). Toss until the peaches are coated, and set aside.

Arrange Peaches:
- Pour the peach mixture into a greased 9x13-inch baking dish, spreading it evenly.

Make Cobbler Topping:

- In a mixing bowl, whisk together flour, sugar, baking powder, and salt for the cobbler topping.

Add Wet Ingredients:
- Add melted butter, milk, and vanilla extract to the dry ingredients. Stir until just combined. The batter will be thick.

Drop Batter on Peaches:
- Drop spoonfuls of the batter over the peaches, covering them as evenly as possible.

Bake:
- Bake in the preheated oven for 40-45 minutes or until the cobbler topping is golden brown and cooked through.

Serve:
- Allow the Peach Cobbler to cool for a few minutes before serving. Serve warm, optionally with a scoop of vanilla ice cream or a dollop of whipped cream.

This Peach Cobbler recipe captures the essence of summer with its juicy peach filling and buttery, slightly crispy cobbler topping. It's a comforting and classic dessert that's perfect for any occasion. Enjoy!

Banana Pudding

Ingredients:

- 3/4 cup granulated sugar
- 1/3 cup all-purpose flour
- 1/4 teaspoon salt
- 3 cups whole milk
- 3 large egg yolks, beaten
- 2 teaspoons vanilla extract
- 3 ripe bananas, sliced
- 1 box (11 ounces) vanilla wafer cookies
- Whipped cream for topping (optional)

Instructions:

Prepare Pudding Base:
- In a medium saucepan, whisk together sugar, flour, and salt. Gradually whisk in the milk until smooth.

Cook Pudding Mixture:
- Cook the mixture over medium heat, stirring constantly, until it thickens and comes to a boil. This will take about 10-12 minutes.

Temper Egg Yolks:
- In a separate bowl, beat the egg yolks. Gradually whisk in about 1 cup of the hot pudding mixture to temper the yolks.

Combine Yolks with Pudding:
- Pour the tempered egg yolk mixture back into the saucepan with the remaining pudding mixture, stirring constantly.

Continue Cooking:
- Cook the pudding for an additional 2 minutes until it thickens. Remove from heat and stir in vanilla extract. Allow the pudding to cool for a few minutes.

Layer Banana Pudding:
- In a serving dish or individual cups, start layering the banana pudding. Begin with a layer of vanilla wafers, followed by a layer of sliced bananas, and then a layer of the pudding. Repeat the layers, ending with a layer of pudding on top.

Chill:

- Cover the banana pudding with plastic wrap, ensuring it touches the surface of the pudding to prevent a skin from forming. Chill in the refrigerator for at least 4 hours or overnight.

Serve:
- Before serving, top the banana pudding with additional vanilla wafers and sliced bananas. Optionally, add a dollop of whipped cream on top.

Enjoy:
- Serve the Banana Pudding chilled and enjoy the creamy, comforting flavors.

This Banana Pudding recipe is a timeless and crowd-pleasing dessert. It's perfect for family gatherings, picnics, or any occasion where you want to share a delicious and comforting treat.

Red Velvet Cake

Ingredients:

For the Cake:

- 2 1/2 cups all-purpose flour
- 1 1/2 cups granulated sugar
- 1 teaspoon baking powder
- 1 teaspoon baking soda
- 1/2 teaspoon salt
- 2 tablespoons unsweetened cocoa powder
- 1 1/2 cups vegetable oil
- 1 cup buttermilk, room temperature
- 2 large eggs, room temperature
- 2 tablespoons red food coloring
- 1 teaspoon vanilla extract
- 1 teaspoon white or apple cider vinegar

For the Cream Cheese Frosting:

- 16 ounces cream cheese, softened
- 1 cup unsalted butter, softened
- 4 cups powdered sugar
- 1 teaspoon vanilla extract

Instructions:

For the Cake:

Preheat Oven:
- Preheat your oven to 350°F (175°C). Grease and flour two 9-inch round cake pans.

Combine Dry Ingredients:
- In a large mixing bowl, sift together flour, sugar, baking powder, baking soda, salt, and cocoa powder.

Mix Wet Ingredients:
- In a separate bowl, whisk together oil, buttermilk, eggs, red food coloring, vanilla extract, and vinegar.

Combine Wet and Dry Mixtures:

- Gradually add the wet ingredients to the dry ingredients, mixing until just combined. Do not overmix.

Divide Batter:
- Divide the batter evenly between the prepared cake pans.

Bake:
- Bake in the preheated oven for 25-30 minutes or until a toothpick inserted into the center comes out clean. Allow the cakes to cool in the pans for 10 minutes before transferring them to a wire rack to cool completely.

For the Cream Cheese Frosting:

Prepare Frosting:
- In a large bowl, beat together cream cheese and butter until smooth and creamy.

Add Sugar and Vanilla:
- Gradually add powdered sugar, beating well after each addition. Stir in vanilla extract.

Frost the Cake:
- Once the cakes are completely cooled, frost the top of one cake layer with a portion of the cream cheese frosting. Place the second cake layer on top and frost the entire cake.

Decorate (Optional):
- Optionally, you can decorate the cake with additional frosting, cake crumbs, or other decorations.

Chill (Optional):
- If desired, chill the cake in the refrigerator for about 30 minutes to allow the frosting to set.

Slice and Serve:
- Slice the Red Velvet Cake and serve. Enjoy!

This Red Velvet Cake is a classic and elegant dessert, perfect for special occasions or as a treat any time of the year. The combination of moist cake and tangy cream cheese frosting is sure to please your taste buds.

Bourbon Bread Pudding

Ingredients:

For the Bread Pudding:

- 8 cups French bread, cut into 1-inch cubes
- 1 cup raisins (optional)
- 4 cups whole milk
- 1 cup heavy cream
- 4 large eggs
- 2 cups granulated sugar
- 1/4 cup bourbon
- 1 tablespoon vanilla extract
- 1/2 teaspoon ground cinnamon
- 1/4 teaspoon ground nutmeg
- Pinch of salt

For the Bourbon Sauce:

- 1/2 cup unsalted butter
- 1 cup powdered sugar
- 1/4 cup bourbon
- 1 teaspoon vanilla extract

Instructions:

For the Bread Pudding:

Preheat Oven:
- Preheat your oven to 350°F (175°C). Grease a 9x13-inch baking dish.

Prepare Bread Cubes:
- Spread the bread cubes evenly in the prepared baking dish. If using raisins, scatter them over the bread cubes.

Mix Custard Mixture:
- In a large mixing bowl, whisk together milk, heavy cream, eggs, sugar, bourbon, vanilla extract, cinnamon, nutmeg, and a pinch of salt until well combined.

Pour Custard Over Bread:

- Pour the custard mixture evenly over the bread cubes, making sure all the bread is soaked. Press down slightly to ensure absorption.

Let it Soak:
- Allow the bread to soak in the custard for about 15-20 minutes.

Bake:
- Bake in the preheated oven for 45-50 minutes or until the bread pudding is set and golden brown on top.

For the Bourbon Sauce:

Prepare Bourbon Sauce:
- In a saucepan, melt butter over medium heat. Stir in powdered sugar, bourbon, and vanilla extract. Cook, stirring constantly, until the sugar is dissolved and the sauce has thickened slightly.

Serve:
- Pour the warm bourbon sauce over individual servings of the bread pudding.

Enjoy:
- Serve the Bourbon Bread Pudding warm, and enjoy the rich, indulgent flavors.

This Bourbon Bread Pudding with Bourbon Sauce is a decadent dessert that's perfect for special occasions or when you want to treat yourself to a delightful Southern classic. The combination of the soft, custardy bread and the warm bourbon sauce is simply irresistible.

Drinks:

Sweet Tea

Ingredients:

- 4-5 black tea bags
- 1 cup granulated sugar (adjust to taste)
- 6 cups water
- Ice cubes
- Lemon slices (optional, for garnish)
- Fresh mint leaves (optional, for garnish)

Instructions:

Boil Water:
- In a medium-sized saucepan, bring 4 cups of water to a boil.

Steep Tea Bags:
- Once the water is boiling, remove it from heat and add the tea bags. Allow the tea bags to steep in the hot water for about 5-7 minutes. The longer you steep, the stronger the tea will be.

Add Sugar:
- While the tea is still hot, stir in the granulated sugar. Adjust the amount of sugar to your desired sweetness level. Stir until the sugar is completely dissolved.

Remove Tea Bags:
- Remove the tea bags from the hot water.

Dilute with Cold Water:
- Pour the sweetened tea concentrate into a heatproof pitcher. Add the remaining 2 cups of cold water to dilute the tea.

Chill:
- Allow the sweet tea to cool to room temperature, then refrigerate until well chilled.

Serve Over Ice:
- Fill glasses with ice cubes and pour the chilled sweet tea over the ice.

Garnish (Optional):
- Garnish the sweet tea with lemon slices and fresh mint leaves if desired.

Enjoy:

- Stir and enjoy the refreshing taste of Southern sweet tea.

Feel free to adjust the sugar level and experiment with the tea-to-water ratio to suit your taste preferences. Sweet tea is a classic and beloved beverage, perfect for sipping on a hot day or as a companion to a delicious Southern meal.

Mint Julep

Ingredients:

- 2 1/2 ounces (75 ml) bourbon
- 8-10 fresh mint leaves, plus a sprig for garnish
- 1/2 ounce (15 ml) simple syrup (adjust to taste)
- Crushed ice

Instructions:

Prepare Mint Leaves:
- Gently muddle the fresh mint leaves in the bottom of a glass. Be careful not to over-muddle, as this can release bitter flavors.

Add Simple Syrup:
- Add the simple syrup to the glass. Simple syrup is made by combining equal parts sugar and water, heated until the sugar dissolves. Allow it to cool before using.

Add Bourbon:
- Pour the bourbon over the muddled mint and simple syrup.

Fill with Crushed Ice:
- Fill the glass with crushed ice. Pack it down to create a frosty exterior on the glass.

Stir:
- Gently stir the ingredients together with a long spoon.

Garnish:
- Top with more crushed ice if needed. Garnish with a sprig of fresh mint.

Serve:
- Serve the Mint Julep immediately while it's ice-cold and refreshing.

The Mint Julep is a quintessential Southern cocktail, and the ritual of sipping it from a frosty silver or pewter cup is part of its charm. Enjoy this classic drink during warm weather or as a festive and elegant choice for special occasions.

Southern Comfort Punch

Ingredients:

- 1 cup Southern Comfort
- 1/2 cup orange liqueur (e.g., triple sec)
- 1 cup pineapple juice
- 1 cup orange juice
- 1/4 cup grenadine
- 1 liter ginger ale, chilled
- Fresh fruit slices (orange, lemon, lime, and/or pineapple) for garnish
- Ice cubes

Instructions:

Prepare the Base:
- In a large punch bowl or pitcher, combine Southern Comfort, orange liqueur, pineapple juice, orange juice, and grenadine. Stir well to mix the ingredients.

Chill:
- Refrigerate the mixture for at least 1-2 hours to allow the flavors to meld and the punch to chill.

Add Ginger Ale:
- Just before serving, pour the chilled ginger ale into the punch bowl or pitcher. Stir gently to combine.

Garnish:
- Add fresh fruit slices to the punch for garnish. You can use slices of oranges, lemons, limes, and/or pineapple.

Serve Over Ice:
- Fill glasses with ice cubes and ladle the Southern Comfort Punch over the ice.

Enjoy:
- Serve the punch immediately and enjoy the fruity and refreshing flavors.

Feel free to customize the recipe to suit your taste preferences. You can also add more or less of the ingredients to adjust the sweetness and strength of the punch. This Southern Comfort Punch is sure to be a hit at your next gathering or celebration. Cheers!

Arnold Palmer (Half-and-Half)

Ingredients:

- 1 cup black tea (brewed and cooled)
- 1 cup lemonade (freshly squeezed or store-bought)
- Ice cubes
- Lemon slices for garnish (optional)
- Fresh mint leaves for garnish (optional)

Instructions:

Brew Tea:
- Brew a cup of black tea following the instructions on the tea packaging. Allow the tea to cool to room temperature.

Prepare Lemonade:
- If you're using freshly squeezed lemonade, combine equal parts fresh lemon juice and cold water, and sweeten with sugar to taste. Alternatively, you can use store-bought lemonade.

Combine Tea and Lemonade:
- In a glass or pitcher, mix equal parts of the brewed black tea and lemonade. You can adjust the ratio to your liking, depending on whether you prefer it more tea-centric or more lemonade-centric.

Add Ice:
- Fill the glass with ice cubes to make the Arnold Palmer extra refreshing.

Garnish (Optional):
- Garnish the drink with lemon slices and fresh mint leaves for an added burst of flavor and a visually appealing touch.

Stir (Optional):
- Give the Arnold Palmer a gentle stir to ensure the tea and lemonade are well mixed.

Serve:
- Serve the Arnold Palmer chilled and enjoy this classic, thirst-quenching beverage.

Arnold Palmer is a versatile drink, and you can easily customize it based on your taste preferences. Some people like to add a splash of simple syrup for extra sweetness, or you can try variations like using green tea instead of black tea. It's a perfect choice for a sunny day or any occasion where you want a refreshing and satisfying beverage.

Mississippi Mudslide (Chocolate Milkshake with Bourbon)

Ingredients:

- 2 cups chocolate ice cream
- 1/2 cup whole milk
- 2 ounces bourbon
- 2 tablespoons chocolate syrup
- Whipped cream for topping
- Chocolate shavings or sprinkles for garnish (optional)
- Maraschino cherry for garnish (optional)

Instructions:

Prepare Ingredients:
- Allow the chocolate ice cream to soften slightly at room temperature for easier blending.

Blend Milkshake:
- In a blender, combine the softened chocolate ice cream, whole milk, bourbon, and chocolate syrup.

Blend Until Smooth:
- Blend the ingredients until smooth and creamy. If the milkshake is too thick, you can add a little more milk and blend again.

Prepare Glass:
- Optionally, drizzle chocolate syrup on the inside of a glass for a decorative touch.

Pour Milkshake:
- Pour the chocolate and bourbon milkshake into the prepared glass.

Top with Whipped Cream:
- Top the milkshake with a generous dollop of whipped cream.

Garnish (Optional):
- If desired, garnish the whipped cream with chocolate shavings or sprinkles. Add a maraschino cherry on top for a classic finishing touch.

Serve:
- Serve the Mississippi Mudslide immediately with a straw or a long spoon for sipping and enjoying.

The Mississippi Mudslide is a luscious and boozy dessert drink that combines the rich flavors of chocolate and bourbon. It's perfect for a sweet indulgence after dinner or as a special treat for chocolate and cocktail enthusiasts. Cheers!

Breakfast/Brunch:

Biscuits and Gravy

Ingredients:

For the Biscuits:

- 2 cups all-purpose flour
- 1 tablespoon baking powder
- 1 teaspoon sugar
- 1/2 teaspoon salt
- 1/2 cup unsalted butter, cold and cut into small pieces
- 3/4 cup buttermilk

For the Gravy:

- 1 pound ground pork sausage (mild or hot)
- 1/4 cup all-purpose flour
- 3 cups whole milk
- Salt and black pepper to taste

Instructions:

For the Biscuits:

Preheat Oven:
- Preheat your oven to 425°F (220°C).

Combine Dry Ingredients:
- In a large bowl, whisk together the flour, baking powder, sugar, and salt.

Add Butter:
- Add the cold, cubed butter to the dry ingredients. Use a pastry cutter or your fingers to cut the butter into the flour mixture until it resembles coarse crumbs.

Add Buttermilk:
- Pour in the buttermilk and stir until just combined. Be careful not to overmix.

Form Dough:

- Turn the dough out onto a lightly floured surface and gently knead it a few times. Pat or roll the dough to a 1/2-inch thickness.

Cut Biscuits:
- Use a biscuit cutter to cut out biscuits from the dough. Place the biscuits on a baking sheet lined with parchment paper.

Bake:
- Bake in the preheated oven for 12-15 minutes or until the biscuits are golden brown on top.

For the Gravy:

Cook Sausage:
- In a large skillet over medium heat, cook the ground pork sausage, breaking it apart with a spoon as it cooks. Cook until browned and cooked through.

Make Roux:
- Sprinkle the flour over the cooked sausage and stir to combine, creating a roux.

Add Milk:
- Gradually add the milk to the skillet, stirring constantly to avoid lumps. Continue to cook and stir until the gravy thickens. Season with salt and black pepper to taste.

Serve:
- Split the warm biscuits in half and ladle the sausage gravy over the top. Serve immediately.

Biscuits and Gravy is a hearty and comforting dish, perfect for breakfast or brunch. It's a true Southern classic that's sure to satisfy your cravings for homestyle comfort food.

Shrimp and Grits Breakfast Casserole

Ingredients:

For the Grits:

- 1 cup stone-ground grits
- 4 cups water
- 1 teaspoon salt
- 2 tablespoons unsalted butter
- 1 cup shredded cheddar cheese

For the Shrimp:

- 1 pound large shrimp, peeled and deveined
- 2 tablespoons olive oil
- 1 teaspoon Cajun seasoning
- Salt and black pepper to taste
- 2 cloves garlic, minced
- 1 tablespoon fresh lemon juice
- 2 tablespoons chopped fresh parsley

For the Casserole:

- 4 large eggs
- 1 cup whole milk
- 1/2 cup heavy cream
- Salt and black pepper to taste
- 1 cup shredded cheddar cheese
- 1/4 cup grated Parmesan cheese
- Chopped green onions for garnish (optional)

Instructions:

For the Grits:

    Cook Grits:

- In a medium saucepan, bring 4 cups of water to a boil. Stir in the grits and salt. Reduce heat to low, cover, and simmer, stirring occasionally, for about 20-25 minutes or until the grits are thick and creamy.

Add Butter and Cheese:
- Stir in the butter and shredded cheddar cheese until melted and well combined. Remove from heat.

For the Shrimp:

Season Shrimp:
- In a bowl, toss the peeled and deveined shrimp with olive oil, Cajun seasoning, salt, black pepper, minced garlic, lemon juice, and chopped parsley.

Cook Shrimp:
- Heat a skillet over medium-high heat. Cook the seasoned shrimp for 2-3 minutes per side or until they are opaque and cooked through. Remove from heat.

For the Casserole:

Preheat Oven:
- Preheat your oven to 375°F (190°C). Grease a 9x13-inch baking dish.

Layer Grits and Shrimp:
- Spread the cooked grits evenly in the bottom of the prepared baking dish. Arrange the cooked shrimp on top of the grits.

Whisk Egg Mixture:
- In a bowl, whisk together eggs, whole milk, heavy cream, salt, and black pepper. Pour this egg mixture over the grits and shrimp.

Add Cheese:
- Sprinkle shredded cheddar cheese and grated Parmesan cheese over the top.

Bake:
- Bake in the preheated oven for 25-30 minutes or until the casserole is set and the top is golden brown.

Garnish:
- If desired, garnish with chopped green onions.

Serve:

- Allow the casserole to cool slightly before slicing and serving. Enjoy your Shrimp and Grits Breakfast Casserole!

This casserole brings together the savory goodness of shrimp and the creamy comfort of grits in a convenient and flavorful dish, perfect for a hearty breakfast or brunch.

Southern-style Breakfast Burrito

Ingredients:

For the Grits:

- 1 cup stone-ground grits
- 4 cups water
- 1 teaspoon salt
- 2 tablespoons unsalted butter
- 1 cup shredded cheddar cheese

For the Southern-style Breakfast Filling:

- 1 tablespoon vegetable oil
- 1/2 pound breakfast sausage, crumbled
- 1 small onion, finely diced
- 1 bell pepper, diced
- 4 large eggs, beaten
- Salt and black pepper to taste
- Hot sauce or salsa (optional, for serving)

For the Burritos:

- Large flour tortillas
- Sliced avocado (optional, for garnish)
- Chopped fresh cilantro (optional, for garnish)

Instructions:

For the Grits:

Cook Grits:
- In a medium saucepan, bring 4 cups of water to a boil. Stir in the grits and salt. Reduce heat to low, cover, and simmer, stirring occasionally, for about 20-25 minutes or until the grits are thick and creamy.

Add Butter and Cheese:
- Stir in the butter and shredded cheddar cheese until melted and well combined. Remove from heat.

For the Southern-style Breakfast Filling:

Cook Breakfast Sausage:
- In a skillet, heat vegetable oil over medium heat. Add crumbled breakfast sausage and cook until browned.

Add Onion and Bell Pepper:
- Add diced onion and bell pepper to the skillet with the sausage. Cook until the vegetables are softened.

Scramble Eggs:
- Push the sausage and vegetables to one side of the skillet. Pour beaten eggs into the skillet and scramble until cooked through.

Combine Filling:
- Mix the cooked eggs, sausage, and vegetables together in the skillet. Season with salt and black pepper to taste.

Assembling the Breakfast Burrito:

Warm Tortillas:
- Heat the flour tortillas in a dry skillet or in the microwave until warm and pliable.

Assemble Burritos:
- Spoon a portion of the grits onto the center of each tortilla. Top with the Southern-style breakfast filling.

Optional Garnishes:
- Garnish with sliced avocado and chopped fresh cilantro if desired.

Fold and Serve:
- Fold the sides of the tortilla over the filling and roll to form a burrito.

Serve with Hot Sauce or Salsa:
- Serve the Southern-style Breakfast Burritos with hot sauce or salsa on the side.

This Southern-style Breakfast Burrito combines creamy grits with a savory breakfast filling, creating a hearty and flavorful meal. Customize the burritos with your favorite toppings and enjoy a taste of Southern comfort for breakfast or brunch.

Grits and Grillades

Ingredients:

For the Grillades:

- 1 1/2 pounds beef or pork round steak, thinly sliced into medallions
- Salt and black pepper to taste
- 1/2 cup all-purpose flour, for dredging
- 4 tablespoons vegetable oil, divided
- 1 large onion, finely chopped
- 1 bell pepper, diced
- 2 celery stalks, diced
- 3 cloves garlic, minced
- 1 can (14 ounces) diced tomatoes, undrained
- 1 cup beef or chicken broth
- 1 teaspoon Worcestershire sauce
- 1 teaspoon Creole or Cajun seasoning (optional)
- Fresh parsley, chopped, for garnish

For the Grits:

- 1 cup stone-ground grits
- 4 cups water
- 1 teaspoon salt
- 2 tablespoons unsalted butter
- 1 cup shredded cheddar cheese

Instructions:

For the Grillades:

Season and Dredge Meat:
- Season the sliced beef or pork with salt and black pepper. Dredge each medallion in flour, shaking off the excess.

Brown Meat:
- Heat 2 tablespoons of vegetable oil in a large, heavy skillet over medium-high heat. Brown the medallions in batches until golden on both sides. Remove the meat and set aside.

Sauté Vegetables:

- In the same skillet, add the remaining 2 tablespoons of oil. Sauté the chopped onion, bell pepper, celery, and garlic until the vegetables are softened.

Add Tomatoes and Broth:
- Stir in the diced tomatoes with their juice. Pour in the beef or chicken broth, Worcestershire sauce, and Creole or Cajun seasoning if using. Bring the mixture to a simmer.

Simmer Grillades:
- Return the browned meat to the skillet, ensuring it's submerged in the liquid. Cover the skillet, reduce the heat to low, and simmer for 1 to 1.5 hours or until the meat is tender and the flavors meld.

Adjust Seasoning:
- Adjust the seasoning with salt and pepper to taste. If the gravy is too thin, you can simmer it uncovered for a bit to thicken.

For the Grits:

Cook Grits:
- In a separate saucepan, bring 4 cups of water to a boil. Stir in the grits and salt. Reduce heat to low, cover, and simmer for about 20-25 minutes or until the grits are thick and creamy.

Add Butter and Cheese:
- Stir in the butter and shredded cheddar cheese until melted and well combined.

Serve:

Assemble:
- Spoon a generous portion of grits onto each plate. Top with grillades and the flavorful gravy.

Garnish and Serve:
- Garnish with chopped fresh parsley and serve the Grits and Grillades while warm.

This Grits and Grillades recipe offers a taste of Southern comfort, combining tender meat with flavorful gravy over creamy, cheesy grits. It's a hearty and satisfying dish that's perfect for a comforting meal.

Louisiana Beignets

Ingredients:

- 1 1/2 cups lukewarm water
- 1/2 cup granulated sugar
- 1 packet (2 1/4 teaspoons) active dry yeast
- 4 cups all-purpose flour
- 1 cup whole milk, at room temperature
- 1/4 cup unsalted butter, melted
- 1 teaspoon salt
- Vegetable oil, for frying
- Powdered sugar, for dusting

Instructions:

Activate Yeast:
- In a mixing bowl, combine lukewarm water and sugar. Sprinkle the active dry yeast over the water and let it sit for about 5-10 minutes until it becomes frothy.

Prepare Dough:
- In a large mixing bowl, combine the activated yeast mixture, flour, milk, melted butter, and salt. Mix until a sticky dough forms.

Knead Dough:
- Turn the dough out onto a floured surface and knead it for about 5 minutes until it becomes smooth. Place the dough in a greased bowl, cover it with a damp cloth, and let it rise in a warm place for 1-2 hours or until doubled in size.

Roll and Cut Dough:
- Once the dough has risen, roll it out on a floured surface to about 1/4-inch thickness. Cut the dough into squares or rectangles.

Heat Oil:
- In a deep fryer or heavy pot, heat vegetable oil to 370°F (188°C).

Fry Beignets:
- Carefully drop a few pieces of dough into the hot oil at a time. Fry until the beignets are golden brown on both sides, flipping them as needed. This should take about 2-3 minutes per batch.

Drain and Dust:

- Remove the fried beignets with a slotted spoon and place them on a paper towel-lined plate to drain excess oil. Immediately dust them generously with powdered sugar while they are still warm.

Serve:
- Serve the beignets warm. They are best enjoyed fresh and hot.

Louisiana Beignets are a delightful treat, and their warm, pillowy texture covered in a sweet layer of powdered sugar makes them a beloved part of Southern cuisine. Enjoy them with a cup of coffee or as a sweet snack anytime!

www.ingramcontent.com/pod-product-compliance
Lightning Source LLC
LaVergne TN
LVHW081557060526
838201LV00054B/1938